HE IS MY SHEPHERD
I AM HIS SHEEP

Dr. Timothy E. Shirley

Edited by Paul Shirley

I would like to dedicate this book to

Doctor Lee Davis, who, as a faithful under-shepherd,

protected the flock, fought the wolves, exposed the

hirelings, and served the Chief Shepherd.

CONTENTS

INTRODUCTION

I have raised sheep for many years. How does a pastor and preacher end up raising sheep? I'm not really sure. My brother Terry, who was a missionary to New York City, actually purchased a Finn ram and brought it back home to me. This was just the beginning of my tenure as a shepherd. The simple reception of a gift from my brother would snowball into a long-term farming experience.

Of course, I soon discovered that owning these animals without knowledge of their care was simply heading for disaster. So I began to read, delving into research to better prepare myself to raise sheep. I ordered literature on lambing. I read books from our local library. I printed everything that I could find on the internet about raising sheep. I slowly started to gain an understanding and knowledge of their needs and care.

That understanding also brought on a sobering realization; I was responsible to meet the needs of these creatures.

I learned to shear them by going to sheep shearing classes. I learned to help deliver lambs by looking at diagrams and reading. I learned to give a lamb an enema when chilled. I learned how to spot the signs of parasites. And, as amazing as it is, I learned to call them by name. Years passed and I began to see each sheep individually. I saw Kate with her gentle and trusting nature. I saw Big Momma with her courage and leadership when walking into a new pasture... It was always interesting to watch the others fall in behind her as she led them through the gaps. I saw Haus with his protective watch care over the ewes. I also saw Stupid (yes, that was her name) with her inability to *ever* calm down. I saw Whitey with her consistent desire to find a hole in the fence and lead others astray. I saw Mouth become the voice of the flock when it was time for them to be fed. And what a voice she had!

Through all of this, I began to gain an understanding of the biblical comparison of "The Good

Shepherd and His Sheep." I would find myself out in the field, simply walking among the flock, thinking about my Shepherd. I would see how much He cared for me each time I assisted a sheep in any way. I would see Him as my Physician whenever I applied medicine to the sick and weak. I would see Him as my Provider whenever I would feed the flock. And there were evenings, as the hot sun would be setting, and the flock would begin to venture out from under the shade to graze, that I would go out in the field and sit among them. Slowly, they would wander over to where I was. I can see in my mind how old Spot would come over to me as I sat there, and she would begin searching for any hidden morsel I might have had for her. She would pull at the sleeve of my shirt and work her nose into the palm of my hand. I would scratch her head and speak to her the entire time, allowing the voice of her shepherd to bring her comfort and peace. As I sat there, I saw *my* Shepherd. More than a Provider, more than a Protector, more than a Physician: He is my friend, one that cares about me personally. He knows me by name.

It is due to this newfound understanding that I decided to write this book, to share what I have learned about sheep, and what that means for the Christian. My hope is that, upon reading this book, you will see what a wonderful thing it is to say these words: He is my Shepherd, and I am his sheep.

CHAPTER ONE

THE INSTINCTS OF SHEEP

The Flocking Instinct.

Sheep love sheep. It's just that simple. It is as natural for a sheep to love another sheep as it is for a mother to love her child. Furthermore, it is instinctive for a sheep to love the flock.

Sheep love to come together. This is not something that the shepherd makes them do; it is a natural desire within a sheep for them to be with other sheep.

They come together to eat. While out in the pasture, the sheep will slowly wander about grazing. Ever so often, I would step out at the fence and throw a treat over to the sheep nearest me. I was always impressed at the ability of the other sheep to know when one of them had gained a treat. I have witnessed fifty head of sheep all milling about in one little spot because of a single apple that was dropped over the fence. They loved the food of the shepherd, and they loved to eat together.

Surely we can see the picture of the Lord's flock in that of the sheep, for we are the sheep of *His Pasture*. We love the food of our Shepherd, and we love to feast together.

O taste and see that the LORD is good: blessed is the man that trusteth in him. (Psalms 34:8)

The time of feasting is a time of joy for the flock. It is a time that is to be desired by those that truly follow the Shepherd. It is for this reason that King David declared:

I was glad when they said unto me, Let us go into the house of the LORD. (Psalms 122:1)

The flock should greatly desire time in church and in fellowship with the brethren. It should not be something that we dread, nor should we find ourselves looking at the clock, wishing for it to end. As I have previously stated: it is instinctive for sheep to desire the fellowship of other sheep.

However, it needs to be said that a sheep will only have this desire for food and fellowship when it is truly under the care of the Good Shepherd. This applies to both the animal and the church member. A church member that is not under the care of the Good Shepherd will not desire the fellowship of the flock, nor the food. I have seen this same scenario played out myself in two ways.

First, there is the sheep that is rebellious to the shepherd. It really is as simple as that. It's a contest of wills: the refusal to submit to the orders of another. I recall a lamb that was not getting sufficient nutrition from its mother's milk. In observing this, I decided to supplement its needs with a bottle, but the lamb refused milk from the bottle. Day by day, I tried my best to get the lamb to eat. I would force open its mouth and watch the milk run down its tongue, but the lamb would simply sull up and refuse to eat. Over time, this lamb's growth was stunted, it's wool was of a poor condition, and it began to be infested with parasites. It is profound to consider that the poor health of this lamb was not due to its lack of milk, for there was an abundance of milk provided. It was not sick due to a lack of attention or care, for both its mother and its shepherd cared for its health. Its poor condition was brought on entirely as a result of its rebellion and refusal to submit to the care and superior knowledge of the shepherd.

Secondly, I would like to consider the sheep that is under a hireling, rather than a shepherd. This is a sheep that is hungry for good food, thirsty for clear water, but there is none provided. Day after day, they are turned out onto the same pasture, one that has long been depleted. There is no growth, no satisfaction. This will cause the sheep to look elsewhere. They will become restless and discontented. Oh, surely we can see the correlation of this picture with our churches today! There is so much discontentment, so much strife. Members are constantly pushing and pulling, trying to gain over another, looking for a better feeling, a higher position, or greater praise. Peaceful, contented fellowship amongst the flock becomes a rarity. Few are the moments of satisfied spiritual feeding, when the brethren commune together in the love of the Savior and the flock, ruminating and growing in peace and harmony. This sort of fellowship and feeding can only be achieved in a place that allows the Good Shepherd to lead, a place that will feed from God's Word as it is, a place where the leaders are following the guidance of the Holy Spirit without their own agendas.

Not only does the flock feed and fellowship together, they also come together to sleep. It is a beautiful sight to see a flock of sheep, all bunched up together in wonderful slumber. They simply love one another and desire the company of their brethren! Take, for example, a flock of sheep lying together in the shade of a single tree on the hottest of days. Instead of spreading out, which would be cooler, they bundle up, practically lying atop one another. They simply *must* stay together. And if they are separated, then the one that has been pulled off from the flock will not be at peace. The only time I have seen a ewe content to be separated from the flock is during lambing season, after the birth. At all other times, a sheep will stand and bleat consistently when separated from the flock.

I believe that this innate desire is reflected in the children of God. God's people simply desire to be with their brethren, to eat and rest from the cares and problems of this life. It greatly concerns me when I hear a professing Christian say, "I don't need the Church. I can serve God right here at home." The issue here is not whether or not you need the church (although every Christian *does*), but rather the issue is whether or not you *want* the church. Church attendance, fellowship with the brethren, and the hearing of the word of God will be a simple, instinctual need that is instilled within the heart of a child of God. I feel that a person who lacks this inward desire is one that has yet to experience a life that is fully submitted to the will of the Shepherd.

It is also important to point out the need that sheep have for one another. A separated sheep will easily fall prey to the many enemies of the flock. It has been witnessed and noted that a flock of sheep will surround an injured lamb and bleat for the shepherd. How divinely the savior has compared us to sheep! Christian friend, there is protection within the flock! If we expect the promises of the Word of God to apply to us, then we must stay within the confines of the Word of God. It is clearly stated in the book of Hebrews chapter ten, verse twenty five:

Not forsaking the assembling of ourselves together, as the manner of some <is>; but exhorting <one another>: and so much the more, as ye see the day approaching.

"*But exhorting one another.*" We, as sheep, need to hear this. Exhortation is to encourage, to embolden, to advise, to give strength and courage. Believe me, this is one commodity that a child of God cannot do without! So you see, not only is it natural for a sheep to be drawn to other sheep, but they *need* one another. The sheep will never find peace until they realize this.

The Instinct Of Light.

And this is the condemnation, that light is come into the world, and men loved darkness rather than light, because their deeds were evil. For every one that doeth evil hateth the light, neither cometh

to the light, lest his deeds should be reproved. But he that doeth truth cometh to the light, that his deeds may be made manifest, that they are wrought in God. (John 3:19-21)

Sheep do not like dark places. They will not willingly go into a stall or pen that does not have adequate lighting. This also is not something that is taught, but it is a natural instinct that sheep have.

It is clearly seen in the scriptures that a child of God will be naturally drawn toward the light, just as sheep are. You will hunger for it, long for it. The darkness will become wearisome to you. You will grow weary of the news, weary of violence, weary of hypocrisy, and weary of the constant turmoil. There will be a yearning in you for that which is *light*.

Light is illumination. In the book of John, chapter three, and verse twenty-one, the Lord Jesus says, "*he that doeth TRUTH cometh to the LIGHT*." Truth and light go hand in hand, for light brings illumination, which reveals truth. He then states, "**that his deeds may be made manifest**." This is clearly the illumination of God over our deeds, to reveal what they *are*. If you look in the previous verses, you will find the contrast. In verses nineteen and twenty, we see the picture of one who hates the light, because it shines on their evil deeds.

Have you ever wondered why an atheist hates God, one whom he claims does not even exist? Why does the atheist hate a bible that someone else is reading? Why does the atheist hate a prayer that someone else is praying? It's because it shines on him. And when it shines on him, he sees himself, and he hates what he sees. But instead of blaming himself and his sinful condition, the atheist blames the light for shining on him and revealing the truth! With a child of God, this is not so. We love the light and are drawn to it! When it shines on us, we bask in its glow. When it reveals our sins, we repent and are thankful for itis illumination. It makes us *better*.

I recently delivered a series of messages on "Spiritual Parasites" in our church. One of those parasites was the spirit of anger. In the process of studying and praying, the light of the word of God shined upon me and revealed to me that I had this parasite in my life. In a moment of illumination, I saw the person that I had become, and I hated it. I hated the way I was making my wife feel. I hated the way I caused my children to dread the thought of approaching me due to my angry spirit. While I wasn't violent or anything like that, I carried an angry spirit that was pushing my family away and causing me to be an unhappy person. But now, having seen it for what it was, I have been able to change. This fact has made our home a better place to be. This improvement is something that does not exist without the light of God's word.

Even more significant to this truth is the concept of loving the Lord Jesus Christ. Seven times in the book of John, our Lord referred to himself as a specific "I Am": I am the good shepherd, I am the bread, I am the resurrection and the life. Then, in chapter nine, He said this:

As long as I am in the world, I am the light of the world. (John 9:5)

And this blessed writer went further with this truth.

This then is the message which we have heard of him, and declare unto you, that God is light, and in him is no darkness at all. (1 John 1:5)

This statement puts this concept into a new context. Since He is the light, when we love the light, we love Him. Since He is the opposite of darkness, if we love darkness, then it is apparent that our love for Him is not what it should be.

John then begins to add to this truth of loving the light and loving Him. He discusses with us the tie of light and fellowship. He first states that, if we have fellowship with the Lord, then we do not walk in darkness.

If we say that we have fellowship with him, and walk in darkness, we lie, and do not the truth: (1 John 1:6)

Of course, this shows us that if we *do* walk in darkness, then we do *NOT* have fellowship with him. Then the question must arise, what is walking in darkness? Let's see what John says:

He that saith he is in the light, and hateth his brother, is in darkness even until now. He that loveth

his brother abideth in the light, and there is none occasion of stumbling in him. But he that hateth his brother is in darkness, and walketh in darkness, and knoweth not whither he goeth, because that darkness hath blinded his eyes. (1 John 2:9-11)

I must admit that I am impressed with John's ability to bind together the love we have for Him, "the light," with the love that we have for the brethren. Isn't it wonderful that a sheep has a desire for other sheep, and a sheep has a desire for light? And isn't it wonderful that the Holy Spirit led John to say, "**He that loveth his BROTHER** (other sheep) **abideth in the LIGHT** (The Lord Jesus)"? How glorious a thought! You can not have one without the other. If you love the light, then you are going to love the brethren. Let us give glory to God for our fellowship with the light and our fellowship with the brethren!

May the Lord help those that have no fellowship with either the brethren nor the Light. They walk in darkness, and they do not even know it. They claim to walk in the light, and yet they hate the brethren. John says this is not so. He says that they *lie*. Truly, the saddest part is their inability to see it! That is why verse eleven states clearly that he knoweth not whither he goeth, because darkness hath blinded his eyes.

Their Instinct To Follow.

And when he putteth forth his own sheep, he goeth before them, and the sheep follow him: for they know his voice. And a stranger will they not follow, but will flee from him: for they know not the voice of strangers. (John 10:4-5)

Sheep are followers. It is in their nature. Many times when I would call my sheep up to lead them into fresh pasture, they would get into a single-file line and walk through the gap. As they would pass through, often the first sheep would jump at the gap, even if there was nothing there to cause this. After the first sheep jumped, the next one would follow suite. This interesting process would go on down the line. It is a common saying, "if you can get one to go then the rest will follow." This is the nature of sheep.

With this understanding comes a significant truth: sheep *need* a shepherd. It is crucial to their survival and health that they have someone to lead them. If left to their own care, they will perish without fail. There can be no other outcome. A sheep without a shepherd is a **dead sheep**.

I recall a particular instance when I sold a few sheep to one of my church members. He lived in a location that was surrounded by woods. The sheep were moved to his barn and put up for the night. Unbeknownst to him, the sheep broke out of the barn shortly thereafter. Instead of staying within the land of their new shepherd, they ventured into the woods. Those sheep were never seen again. There is no doubt in my mind that they are now dead. It is a simple but significant truth that a sheep left to itself will die.

So, not only do sheep need other sheep, but sheep need a *shepherd*. They are designed to know *how* to follow, and they know *who* to follow: sheep know the voice of the shepherd as well as the sound of their own flock. It has been of great interest to visitors and preachers that come to my home to witness me calling my sheep. As I would step out from my home and look over the fields, there they would be, scattered out and grazing without a care in the world. I would walk up to the fence, giving a loud and solid call, "HUPP!" This would cause them all to immediately stop grazing and raise their heads to find my position. Following my lead, I would have the visitor mimic my sheep-call. Giving it their best shot, they would call out a clear "HUPP!" The sheep would ignore them completely, going back to grazing. I would then give them another solid "HUPP." Once again, gain their attention. Then I would call out twice in succession, "HUPP HUPP" and here they would come, running forward as if in a race. The shepherd had called. They would come close, milling around to see what I had for them. It was always something I enjoyed doing.

The Lord knew this. And He knew that we, as His sheep, would know His voice. WE KNOW HIS VOICE! There is no confusion to His call. There is no question to His call. His leadership and His guidance are clear and decisive. Many times I have heard Christians make a statement that I do not think is correct: "I know that God wants me to do something, I just don't know what it is." Although I understand that the person in this statement is seeking the will of God, it implies that the Lord is not leading them. They are drawing a picture of a God that has a plan for them, one who is *telling* them that He has a plan for them, but will not show them *what that plan is*. I do not think that the problem here is the Lord's unwillingness to reveal His will. The problem is their unwillingness to follow! God wants to see us simply graze where He has placed us, to wait upon His clear and decisive call, and to trust in his wisdom and leadership. He wants us to serve wherever He has placed us with a thankful heart and be patient. I have had many church members come to me with a request, desiring to be used in some area of ministry, but these same Christians have yet to show themselves faithful in the simple things, such as prayer and study of God's word. They are yet to follow their Shepherd to the church to be fed. How can we expect the Lord to lead us into the larger areas of importance when we haven't even learned to follow Him in the simple things?

Furthermore, the leadership of the shepherd places the responsibility of the sheep completely on *His* shoulders. When my flock needed to be moved, it was my responsibility to lead them to an area where they could grow. It was not the responsibility of the sheep, they were simply supposed to follow. After I would move them, then it would be my responsibility to decide how long they were to stay there before being moved again. It was not necessary for the sheep to approach me each time I came to the field to ask me if it was time to move yet. Wouldn't that be something, If every time I went into the flock the sheep all gathered around and asked me, "should we move to another field yet? Is it time? Have I been here to long?" Instead of grazing and growing, they would waste their time fretting about the timing and location of their next move. But *we* do this! How many Christians have missed the blessings of the pasture where the Shepherd has placed them because they were too preoccupied with moving on?

Sometimes, a sheep comes along that is not willing to follow the shepherd. These are the ones that walk the edge of the field, looking for a gap in the fence.

No matter how green the grass is, or how clear the water may be, it is never good enough for its contentment. I have witnessed this again and again with the same ewes. There was one sheep particular that I named "Houdini" due to this annoying trait. Whenever I would bring the flock into the barn, she would always push at the door. When I put them into a fresh field, she would walk the perimeter seeking for a hole for escape.

This was unhealthy for that sheep. In her desire to disobey me, she was constantly getting hurt. Once, she ripped off a piece of her ear while trying to go through a hole that was much too small for her. There was feed provided just inches from her nose, but she would rather escape than eat. She did not trust the leadership of her shepherd. She did not agree with the contentment of the rest of the flock, and she never realized the damage that she was doing to herself. With a sheep like this, the shepherd will use control, hoping that a change will take place. And that is what I did. I put her in places where there was no escape, hoping for willing submission. I placed her in a position of dependence by making myself her only source of water and food, all in a desire to bring her into submission. I wanted to be her shepherd, and I wanted her to be my sheep. I knew what she needed, and I knew that she was only hurting herself. The only way to help her was for her to follow me.

What a lesson this is for us to retain! Our shepherd does not want us to follow Him because He is some power-hungry tyrant that demands obedience. He is not trying to extinguish our freedom or our right to express ourselves; He desires to protect us, to keep us from hurting ourselves! He desires to lead the young lady away from the destructive relationship, to lead the young man away from the influence of drugs and alcohol, to lead the parent away from the destructive power of sin and the flesh. He does not do this to punish us, but to bless us. I know that this statement is not appreciated, but God does these things for our own good. He knows what we need, and when one of His sheep refuses to follow Him, He will attempt to gain their submission in much the same way that a human shepherd will. He will place that sheep in a position of dependence, in a place where there is no one to turn to but Him. He does this in a desire to win the sheep to Himself. The book of James gives us a beautiful picture of this truth:

> *My brethren, count it all joy when ye fall into divers temptations; Knowing this, that the trying of your faith worketh patience. But let patience have her perfect work, that ye may be perfect and entire, wanting nothing. (James 1:2-4)*

In this passage, we are given an unusual piece of advice: "count it all joy when ye fall into divers temptations." The word "divers" implies that there are many different kinds of temptations. Temptation here does not refer to the lust of the flesh, but the trials that come our way. We can clearly see that in the next verse. The writer is telling us that, when we fall into many different trials, we should count it a *joy*. Imagine that, someone telling us that it is a joyous occasion when we are going through a hard time... Now, look at verse three and see why it is a joyous occasion:

> *Knowing this, that the trying of your faith worketh patience.*

James is stating that, while we are in the trial, we know something: this is a trying of our faith. We also know that this trying will work patience in us. It will cause us to have to wait. We will be dependent on Him. We will be patient by faith. And when we are patient by faith, then verse four happens:

But let patience have her perfect work, that ye may be perfect and entire, wanting nothing.

Do you see? It is a perfect work that He is doing in us! He places us in a position of dependency to Him so that we may learn to trust in Him. He then brings us through the trial and does a perfect work in us. Notice the end result of His trial: "that we may be perfect and entire, wanting nothing." The trial did not damage us. It did not leave us scarred for life. It made us entire, whole, and wanting nothing. It left us *satisfied*. This is the desire of the Shepherd when dealing with a sheep that does not follow Him.

Still, even with such care from the shepherd, sometimes a sheep just will not submit. I recall a particular spring after the lambs had all been born, and the early grass had broken through the soil. I had already walked the fence and prepared the pasture for the first grazing of the year. The field was clean, and the feast was ready. I opened the door of the barn and watched as the flock went forth for their first bite of green grass. The mother ewes were calling to their lambs as they ventured out into the fields, and the lambs were all calling back. The young ewes that were filled with energy were leaping into the air with the joy that comes from the ending of winter and the newness of spring. The old ewes were easing along and stopping at the first clump of grass they could find. What a wonderful time this was! And then I spotted Houdini. She made her way to the edge of the fence, considering its strength. She then called to her lamb and went forth along the fence line, periodically testing it. After a few weeks, I noticed Houdini not only had her lamb following her, but many other lambs were also taking an interest in her leadership. She would lead them around the fence, sticking her head into every hole she could find. Of course, the lambs did the same. It wasn't long before I found one of those lambs outside of the fence, dead from the attack of a dog. Had that lamb stayed within the perimeters of the fence, it would have lived. But because it "escaped," it suffered an unnecessary and untimely death. It went where it did not need to go. And the influence of Houdini was the cause of it all.

At that point, I was faced with a desperate decision. As a shepherd, I desire an abundance of health and life for every sheep, but I am responsible for the entire flock. At that point, I had an element within my flock that was endangering the lives of the young ones. I was left with no choice, no other recourse. As soon as her lamb was weaned, I took her to the slaughterhouse. I found no joy in it, but I was certain that my decision was the correct one. A hard choice had to be made for the good of the entire flock.

In the book of First Corinthians chapter five, the Apostle Paul states that he had received reports of fornication among the brethren. He also said that they were "puffed up" and not sorrowful for their deeds. This tells me they had been given the opportunity to repent and submit to the leadership of the Lord, but instead they were puffed up, rebellious, and obstinate. He then instructs the Church to gather together and to turn this rebel over to the devil for the destruction of the flesh. This is the slaughterhouse. In verse six, he explains the urgency for this drastic measure:

> **Your glorying is not good. Know ye not that a little leaven leaveneth the whole lump? (1 Corinthian 5:6)**

Surely we can all see the warning that is given in this passage. It is no small thing to bring rebellion to the shepherd within the flock. A little leaven leaveneth the whole lump. There needs to be a realization of the impact that our rebellion has on the rest of the flock, especially the young ones! Let us be willing to be His sheep, and let us allow Him to be our Shepherd. This will bring peace within the flock.

Who the sheep follows is dependent upon whom the sheep trust. My flock trusts me because I feed them. I spend time with them, and they know me. When the storm is coming, I call them into the shelter of the barn. When the grass is gone, and the flock is hungry, I provide them with feed and hay. When a ewe is giving birth, I stand by her and assist when needed. I am involved in their lives. This is a trust that is earned. And just as I have earned the trust of my flock, surely we could all agree that our Shepherd has earned our trust as well. He has been as faithful to meet the need of His flock as any shepherd could be. He has been there in our times of hunger, and He has provided. He has given us sweet comfort during the times of the blackest storms. He has loved us when we felt that no one loved us. We've been given companionship, comfort, and counsel. He has never left us! He has earned our trust. And yet, sometimes we respond to Him as if we do not trust Him. It is as if we believe that we know the location of green grass more than He does. When it comes down to it, it's a simple matter of who you trust, in whom you place your confidence. Who do you believe really knows the best way for you to go? It is a true statement that sheep are followers, but who they follow will depend on who they trust. Let me encourage you, dear reader, to put your trust in the Good Shepherd. He knows where He is going, and He knows what you need.

The Instinct For Pasture.

Sheep love to go through a new gate into fresh pasture. It is a wondrous sight to see as a flock of sheep move from one field to another into some tall, green grass. They will run and jump while kicking their back legs over their heads. It is a display of sheer joy. This is a time of excitement for the sheep, but it is also a time of joy for the shepherd. It is always a treat for the shepherd to see his flock's excitement as he calls them up for new pasture. In fact, the sheep generally know what the call of the shepherd is about depending on his location. For instance, if I am at the barn when I call, they know that they will be fed in the barn. If I am at the watering trough, then they know that the call is for water. When I walk out into the field and open the gap into fresh pasture, they know that this is something else. I like to stand at the gap and call them up without opening the gate until they are all there. I will stand there and call, "HUPP HUPP." There are always those that are younger and faster that make it to the gap first, but I wait.

I remember an old sheep I had for years that was coming down to her last days. I would make the call, and she would faithfully turn and begin the journey to where I was. The rest of the flock would be standing there, anxious to get through, but I would wait. She had been a faithful sheep and an excellent mother. She deserved the fresh pasture as much as the young. After a short time, she would arrive and I would let them all through. As I opened the gap, the young ones would run in at full steam. The older ones would just step over into the fresh pasture and put their noses to the ground. There was no rush, there was no need for pushing or shoving. The shepherd had brought them to a place of pasture, and there would be plenty for all.

I believe it is important for us, as His sheep, to recognize our need to move on to new pasture, to be led into new areas of growth. As a pastor, I have learned that it is crucial to the health and growth of a church to regularly find new pasture. Equally so, as I observe the churches that appear to be quietly fading away, I can clearly see the absence of growth and new pasture in their past.

There is an epidemic of complacency that is creeping through many of our churches. I am seeing a lack of excitement or even *desire* for true spiritual growth. A flock that does not experience the leadership of the shepherd into new pasture is a flock that is doomed to die. As I previously stated, it is absolutely crucial for the sheep to go into these fresh pastures, for their health and growth. This is meant to be a time of excitement and joy for them as well. However, without this growth and movement, a flock becomes stagnant, like a pond with no fresh water.

The vision of the flock is to be led into fresh pasture, and this vision is essential for life in the flock.

Where there is no vision, the people perish: but he that keepeth the law, happy is he. (Proverbs 29:18)

The shepherd knows this. Whether it is the Good Shepherd (our Lord) or an under-shepherd (a pastor), he must be aware of the need of the flock to continually move to new pasture.

> **For he \<is\> our God; and we \<are\> the people of his pasture, and the sheep of his hand. To day if ye will hear his voice, (Psalms 95:7)**

Of course, we do not have to worry about the Lord Jesus doing *His* job of leadership. He is always faithful. However, the same cannot be said for those of us that are in the pastorate. Pastors can become lazy, routinely going into every service and preaching on the same things, in the same way, at the same time in every meeting. Over time, the congregation will become numb and lose interest. We have the same sort of revivals at the same time each year, with the same speakers saying the same things, and often times the men that stand to deliver the word have not studied nor sought the leadership of the Lord. It is due to this lack of sincere effort and work coming from the pulpit that many of our congregations are dying out. There are no new births, no excitement, and no desire. There is no vision of going into a new pasture. We are satisfied with the way things are, and we don't want to shake things up. We have settled into our comfort zones. This is dangerous and detrimental to the flock! Let me encourage every church member to desire growth and new pasture, and every pastor to faithfully follow the Good Shepherd: He will lead you into fresh, green pasture.

A few years ago, I was sitting behind the pulpit of our church at the beginning of the service when I felt an impression from the Lord on my heart and mind. As I meditated on the direction I was receiving from God, I began to understand that He was leading me to start a new ministry within our church. The time had come to take a new step of growth, and my Shepherd wanted me to lead them in it. I cannot recall if something was said in the service that spurred this direction of thinking or if it simply came to me, but I knew that the Lord wanted our church to launch a jail ministry. This was something that I had never done. I didn't even know where to start, but I stepped up to the pulpit and shared my vision with the congregation. Just like a flock of sheep heading into new pasture, the congregation immediately became excited. Following the service, I was approached by several members expressing their desire to participate in this new venture. Since that time, countless men and women have been saved due to this ministry. Now we are regularly holding church services and revivals in several local jails. One of the preachers in our church surrendered to the mission field and is now a missionary to the jails of the state of Kentucky. He has also accepted the position of Chaplain in one of the correctional facilities where he often ministers.

Over the years, the Lord has periodically led us into these new pastures, from the work of missions to youth rallies. Each time a new gate is presented, we walk through it. The young are jumping and leaping, the elder stepping in with faith and assurance. This is the leadership of our Shepherd, and it will be wonderful. Even in the messages I preach to our church each week, I have come to understand that the Lord leads me to take specific directions, to lead the congregation into new areas of growth. Sometimes it is practical living with such things as faith, patience and the like. Other times it concerns the understanding of biblical prophecy. I find myself leading the church through various series of messages that appear to have a focused intent within them that the Lord wants them to learn. Pastors that preach the same things each Sunday will learn that the congregation needs to move on! They need to be led into fresh new pasture, else they will grow stagnant, which leads to sickness.

CHAPTER TWO

THE HEALTH OF SHEEP

A healthy sheep is a happy sheep. And the health of a sheep is dependent on preventive measures. Any shepherd worth their salt will work to prevent the sheep from getting sick. It can be extremely difficult to help a sheep that has become very sick. They do not have much of a will to live once they reach a certain point. Therefore, the best practices at the shepherd's disposal are preventive measures. They must be fed right, doctored right, and cared for continually in order for success; a neglected flock will become a sick one.

In this chapter, I would like to look deeper at some practices that will keep the flock healthy. This should be beneficial to any Christian who is following their Lord, as well as to any pastor striving to be a good under-shepherd.

The Nutrition Of A Sheep.

Nutrition completely controls the performance of a flock. This statement is profound in its application. The concept of our performance and success being dependent on what we eat is one that merits thorough consideration. Just as a sheep must have the proper nutrition in order to be beneficial to its shepherd, so must a believer have the proper spiritual nutrition in order to become beneficial. I do not know how we have missed this in our spiritual lives, but we have. The importance of nutrition has become so prevalent in our society when it concerns our flesh that you can hardly step into a grocery store without seeing it portrayed. Eat right, exercise, watch your fats, build strong bones, take your vitamins, proper diet and nutrition has become a dominant message in our day. But for some reason, we have failed to see the importance of applying this truth to our spiritual well-being. If we would simply stop and compare the need of proper physical nutrition to our need of proper *spiritual* nutrition, then we would undoubtedly agree that we are not eating right. We miss meals, eat the wrong things, eat too much of one thing while leaving out another, and then we assume that we will be strong and healthy enough to face the day. Friend, it is simply not so! Most Christians have become weak, anemic, and are suffering from spiritual malnutrition!

Chewing the Cud. What a term this is. It refers to a process of eating in certain animals, like sheep. They chew their food once before regurgitating it in the form of "cud," and then they repeat the chewing process to thoroughly break down the food for digestion. Another word for this is to "ruminate." It is a slow process that promotes growth and health in sheep. For the shepherd, watching a sheep lie down and chew the cud is an encouraging experience. This is good for the production of flesh, fat, fleece, and milk. It is a scene that I have enjoyed many times. In the early morning hours, the flock will have their noses to the ground looking for the choicest of blades, searching for the sweet grasses that they love. They will do this until the sun rises high, and then they'll head for the shade. As they all find a spot to rest, they settle in until evening. And then, one by one, they begin to chew with the nice, slow, drawn-out movement of their jaws as they would bring what they had already eaten that morning back up. They would chew that segment of cud until it had exhausted it's nutrients and then swallow it into another compartment of their stomach. The sheep would then bring more of the morning's grazing back up to repeat the process. It is truly a sight to see when the entire flock is lying under the shade, looking like a group of animals chewing bubble gum!

This is the process of a sheep's digestion. It is a slow process that involves rumination. It's not a quick fix, not fast food. It's a slow, dedicated thing. Surely we can see the lesson. Our food is the Bible, God's Holy Word. There is no quick-fix meal from it. It is a book to be read, then meditated upon. Many complain today of their lack of understanding as they read the Bible. I fear we have become so spoiled in our fast-paced society that anything requiring dedication becomes too hard, too much work. What we don't realize is, this is the way of a sheep. The Bible lays out our process of learning and growing through His word:

> **Whom shall he teach knowledge? and whom shall he make to understand doctrine? <them that are> weaned from the milk, <and> drawn from the breasts. For precept <must be> upon precept, precept upon precept; line upon line, line upon line; here a little, <and> there a little: (Isaiah 28:9-10)**

In verse nine, we see the need to teach knowledge and doctrine, but only to those that have been weaned from the milk. Doctrine is not for the babe, for surely they need to grow quickly at first. It is for this reason that we often see a new convert grow by leaps and bounds for a short time. But after a time, when they are strong enough, they are weaned. Then comes the time of growth.

Now, in verse ten, we are presented with the proper order of our learning. "Precept upon precept." A precept is a command or ordinance. These precepts are the very ideas and concepts of Christianity. The biblical precepts define who we are and what we believe. These are the first things that we are taught after we are saved and begin to grow. We are given the precepts of Baptism, Communion, Church membership, etc.

Next, this verse says "line upon line." These are our steps into the scriptures. Slowly but surely, we begin a journey into the Word of God. We learn of the creation, of the flood, and the call of Abraham. We learn of Isaac and Jacob, who had twelve sons. We learn of the nation called Israel and its significance. Line upon line, we learn, and we continue doing this until we gain a general understanding of it all.

Then our verse says, "here a little, and there a little." As we grow, we ruminate. We become in-depth in our studies. Our minds and our hearts ponder the mysteries of the Word of God, and we hunger for more. The grazing that we have done in the mornings, as we enjoy our time of devotion, becomes our ruminant through the day as we chew every ounce of nutrition that we can get from each bite. This is the way of a sheep. David was a shepherd, and he understood this truth. Look at the first words of the psalmist in his writings:

Blessed is the man that walketh not in the counsel of the ungodly, nor standeth in the way of sinners, nor sitteth in the seat of the scornful. But his delight is in the law of the LORD; and in his law

doth he meditate day and night. And he shall be like a tree planted by the rivers of water, that bringeth forth his fruit in his season; his leaf also shall not wither; and whatsoever he doeth shall prosper. (Psalm 1:1-3)

David shows us that a man is blessed when, rather than walking in the counsel of the ungodly, or standing in the way of sinners, or sitting in the seat of the scornful, he delights in the law of the Lord, and *he meditates on it day and night*! This is rumination.

Now, notice what happens to this man that meditates. He shall be like a tree that bringeth forth his fruit in his season. His leaf shall not wither. Whatsoever he doeth shall prosper. This is growth, and this is health. Again, this is the way of sheep! Our health and growth depend on the process of rumination. We *must* meditate upon His Word. We must learn it precept upon precept, line upon line, here a little and there a little. I cannot emphasize enough the need for our churches to push the Word of God, to teach it in Sunday School and to preach it in worship! It is vital to the health of the flock. There is no substitute. It is a slow process that takes a lifetime, but it is *not* monotonous. The more I learn, the more I hunger. The deeper I delve, the further I want to go. It is a wondrous journey, to learn the bible, and I want more of it.

The Tablelands. The high tablelands of Israel were a source of nourishment for the flocks. These spots were located on the tops of mounts. However, rather than a peak, the tops of these mounts would have flat, lush fields of grass perfectly fit for the flocks. In order for the shepherd to take his flock to these areas, he would first take several precautions.

First, he would scout the area for vipers and predators. He would also scan the growth for anything poisonous that the flock might eat accidentally. After securing the area, he would lead his sheep to the pasture so that they could feast. It is with this scene in mind that the Psalmist David wrote these words:

Thou preparest a table before me in the presence of mine enemies: thou anointest my head with oil; my cup runneth over. (Psalms 23:5)

There, in the midst of the wilderness, the shepherd would abide with his sheep. All around the flock would be the dangers of the world, but here, in this place of nourishment, the sheep could graze without a care, without fear. The sheep could feast on the grass of the high country. And may I say, there is just something about that grass, to reach a place of fellowship with the Shepherd that is higher than anything a man can find in this world… What a joy and privilege to go beyond self, to go beyond flesh, and to experience the sweetness of His presence. Once you reach *this* place, it does not magnify the man: it magnifies the Lord.

He must increase, but I must decrease. (John 3:30)

In my experience, I have found that many Christians believe that "feasting on the high ground" has something to do with an elevated feeling of spirituality. Now, I don't want to belittle genuine praise, nor the exaltation of the glory that can fill the soul of the believer, but to *truly* feast on the grass of the high tableland is *so much more* than that. It is to be *near Him*, to experience His protection while you feast on His word and guidance. It is to learn something of yourself and desire to change. It is to have a nugget of gold revealed to you while looking into His Word. And it is to *grow*. So many today have missed this! We are so wrapped up in entertainment, even in our churches, that we have become shallow and malnutritioned. We no longer see the need to faithfully attend church or Sunday school. If there is a big event taking place, then many will attend, because it's exciting and new. But to find yourself calmly feasting on the Word of God with the presence of the Shepherd near? *That is true nourishment.* To have Him speak to your soul through His word, to hear His voice while listening to your pastor, to understand His touch of peace while you're surrounded by the dangers of the world... These are the personal touches that seem to be lacking in the lives of the believers. When you know this kind of fellowship and nourishment, you will know the joy that is unspeakable and full of glory! And that joy brings thankfulness: for you are His sheep, and He is your shepherd.

Balance. For healthy nutrition in sheep, it is also necessary to have balance. In order for a sheep to remain healthy, they must have more than sweet feed. Of course, sheep love the sweet feed. They will take it from anyone.

Some time ago, I received a call from a school teacher asking if she could bring her class to the farm to see my sheep. This was a class of four year olds. I suppose you would call it pre-school. In order for these little ones to be able to see the sheep up close, I felt it would be good to put the flock in the barn. And so I did. It was interesting to watch as these children came into the barn. They were enthralled by the sheep. They kept climbing up on the gates and trying to enter the stalls. They did so with no fear of being trampled or hurt. Of course, the flock began to be in great distress. Every sheep ran to the back wall of the stall and remained there with a watchful eye. Seeing the children's desire to touch the sheep, I decided to get a bucket of feed. Each child was given a small portion in their hand and was instructed to hold out the feed between the bars of the gate. As they did so, a few of the sheep caught the scent of the feed. Immediately they came forward to eat. First only two came, then four, then more. Before long, I had an entire class of four year olds running to the bucket to get more feed then running to the gate to feed an awaiting sheep. This went on until I decided that the sheep had had enough. Although the sheep didn't know it, and although the children could not understand it, I knew the flock did not need any more: too much of the sweet feed would make them sick.

When I think of sweet feed, I think of the things that we enjoy, those things that come easy to us as believers, such as gospel singings and services of praise. These are the spiritual things that we enjoy. We are on board for a revival once or twice a year, with a new evangelist and special singing. Of course, there is nothing wrong with these things, but we need *more than that*. A sheep must also have **roughage**. Now, roughage consists of the stems of grass and hay that sheep eat when they graze. It is very important for the digestion of a sheep that they regularly consume this roughage. As it's not as sweet or easy to eat, sheep must put forth effort to eat this. They have to graze, or they have to approach the hay manger and pull out the hay. And they must *chew*. This is not a food that is simple to eat. It takes effort and persistence. Can you see the lesson?

Considering the blessedness of the tablelands, we must also see the necessity of it: to eat roughage, to partake of that which is not so easily attained but is very beneficial. A sheep that does not get this roughage along with their feed will *bloat*. It'll swell up and die. The feed will pack in their gut, and the sheep will not be able to digest it. I have witnessed this many times in the lives of believers that only feed on music and spiritual highs. When it came time to settle in and eat, they lost interest. This pattern continued until even the sweet feed was no longer desirable!

However, I have also witnessed a new convert settle in and begin to grow by feasting on the Word. I have seen this convert sit on the front seat with a bible open in their lap as I would deliver the message of God. I have watched as this convert would begin to ruminate and grow. Then, when the times of the sweetness came along, the health and growth of this sheep caused the experience to be even better. When a sheep grows properly, the sweet feed never becomes undesirable. The sweet feed is always good to the sheep that practices balance. Let me encourage you to settle into a church that preaches and teaches the King James Bible. Learn and grow! Feast on the Word of God, both the sweetness and the roughage of it. Read it and pray. It will take dedication, it will take effort, but you will experience spiritual health and growth that will never regret. Attend your church faithfully. Pay attention to the messages. Eat the roughage. Ruminate and meditate. If you will give time to proper spiritual nutrition, then you will experience the feast of the tableland with the Shepherd.

Water and Minerals are also essential to the health and well-being of the flock. We have an understanding of the need for water, but there is an interesting connection between water and minerals that we should consider.

First of all, a sheep needs water. It is an absolute *necessity*. Due to the heat of their bodies and the wool that they carry, their need for water is greater than other animals. Therefore, it is important for a shepherd to make sure that his flock has adequate watering facilities. The flock should never have to travel more than ½ mile to get drinkable water. There needs to be an accessible watering facility near the flock at all times. Whenever they need a drink, a drink should be provided.

Water is a type of the word of God. We know this from the scriptures:

That he might sanctify and cleanse it with the washing of water by the word, (Ephesians 5:26)

With this in mind, we can see the message clearly. We, His sheep, need water, which is the Word. It is absolutely necessary to our health. I realize that I have addressed this in previous points, but I would like to take a moment to focus on the availability of the Word. As I have said, a sheep should never have to travel over ½ mile to get water. So it is with us as His sheep. Our churches should be wonderful watering-holes for all believers. It is a shame that so many sheep are depending upon a television evangelist or some other outer-means to quench their thirst. I do not believe this was ever the intent of the Lord for His church. The local church is meant to be a place of nourishment for the flock! The Word of God needs to flow from the pulpit. It needs to flow from the Sunday school rooms. It needs to flow from Bible studies and special services. We need more than just a superficial reading of the scriptures; we need a deep, in-depth study that will quench the harshest of thirsts. I fear that the shallowness in our pulpits and classes have caused our flocks to look elsewhere to quench their thirst. Pastors and teachers desperately need to see the importance of their positions! The flock depends on the water of the Word for restoration. This is why David wrote, "He leadeth me beside the still waters. He restoreth my soul." After being out in the hot, blistering heat of the world, a sheep needs the restorative drink of the Word of God. It is the only thing that will suffice! I say, give me a cool drink drawn from the deep-end of the Book. Show me something that I have not seen and restore my soul. Quench my thirst with a refreshing draught of His Word that will satisfy all the way down.

Minerals go with water. A flock will drink more water if they are given an endless supply of salt and minerals. So, salt will cause a sheep to desire more water, and the water will be sweeter and more satisfying. We also know that salt is a preservative. To help us gain an understanding of the spiritual application, let us consider the following verse:

And grieve not the holy Spirit of God, whereby ye are sealed unto the day of redemption. (Ephesians 4:30)

The Holy Spirit is our preservative. He seals us unto the day of redemption. If we consider the connection in this thought, then it becomes clear: the seasoning of the Holy Spirit will give us a thirst for the word of God. For it is through the Holy Spirit that the Word of God comes alive to the believer. He makes it new and fresh to us. Therefore, to be filled with the Spirit will greatly influence your desire for the Word. Equally so, to be filled with the *flesh* will bring on a callousness and disinterest toward the Word of God. As a pastor, I often witness this firsthand. It is not difficult to see those that have the Holy Spirit working in their lives. When it is time for preaching, they focus in with anticipation.

On the other hand, it is not difficult to recognize those that lack a presence of the Holy Spirit in their lives. They seem to have the ability to completely ignore the man standing behind the pulpit delivering the scriptures.

Sunday school is not important to them, nor is any other service that involves learning. It is not an activity that the flesh enjoys.

And further, by these, my son, be admonished: of making many books <there is> no end; <u>and much study <is> a weariness of the flesh.</u> (Ecclesiastes 12:12)

It is absolutely crucial to the health of a sheep that it gets enough water. Furthermore, the intake of minerals like salt contributes to the sheep's desire to drink. It is equally crucial to the health of the Lord's sheep that it gets an ample supply of the Word of God, and the presence of the Holy Spirit working in our lives will contribute to our desire for His Word.

And be not drunk with wine, wherein is excess; <u>but be filled with the Spirit:</u> (Ephesians 5:18)

Minerals prevent sickness in a sheep. Each spring, when the new grass is growing rapidly, there is a danger of a sheep getting grass tetany. This comes as a result of a mineral deficiency. I have seen this many times as a ewe would begin to show a stiffness in the way she would walk. Over time, her condition would worsen to the point that I would become concerned. She would lie down, only to stand right back up. She just couldn't get settled and rest. After this, she would start to stagger, much like a drunken man, and her eyes would dart from side to side. This deficiency would affect her milk production to the point of depletion, which could harm the lamb. I have had to literally carry a ewe back to the barn, because she had not received enough minerals in her diet to prevent this from happening. Quite often, the sheep would also be dehydrated from a lack of water. This sickness requires a large dosage of medicine to quickly offset the symptoms. If this is not done, then the sheep would not be able to cope with the stress put on her body, and she would certainly die.

As I remember these times with my flock, I can see the correlation between them and us, the Lord's sheep. Viewing earthly minerals as a type of the Holy Ghost, we can grasp the lesson. The stiffness in the sheep from the lack of minerals is just the beginning. Right now, I can see in my mind the faces of members that have developed a stiffness in *their* walk. It is not an extreme change, but a subtle one. Sure, they are still attending the services, still going through the motions, still walking with the rest of the flock, but there is a hesitation to their willingness and a lack of desire for the Word. Eventually, they will become restless, never settled, never content. Their deficiency is progressing. The lack of the Word and the Holy Spirit is now affecting them. Just as the mineral-deficient sheep eventually loses control over their own bodies, so it is with the Lord's sheep; We begin to stagger like drunken men with no discretion or restraint. With darting eyes, we look here and there. The young ones who depend upon us to supply their needs are left without... It's a terrible sight to see. If something is not done, then spiritual death is imminent. Sometimes, even a physical death can occur as a result of this deficiency.

We, his sheep, must have the Word of God seasoned with the Holy Spirit if we are to be healthy productive sheep. If you see the signs of this deficiency coming on, then I exhort you to find yourself in prayer before Him. Repent of any hindrances, and request a renewal of your desire for His Word with a fresh touch of His presence.

Proper Maintenance of Sheep.

A good shepherd will practice **preventive maintenance**. This means they will do everything they can to prevent the sheep from getting sick to start with. It is much more profitable and productive to keep sheep healthy than it is to fight some sickness that can spread throughout the entire flock. If you consider a sheep's willingness to give up, it is dangerous to allow one to become sick at all. I have witnessed several healthy ewes fall into a stupor due to sickness. They quit eating, drinking, and then walking because of a small sickness that they had contracted. Once a sheep gets down, it is difficult to ever get them back up again. Oh, it can be done, but it is never easy, and it takes constant vigil mixed with persistence.

I cannot help but wonder how many pastors would see a connection between this truth and the church members they know. I'm certain that they could recall a member of the flock who walked down into a place of darkness, ignoring the warnings of the Bible, ignoring the voice of the shepherd, where they contracted some sickness due to their carelessness. That's bad enough, but then we can see their willingness to give up… They can't see the point in going on. Then one problem becomes two, then four, and so on. In the end, you wind up with a sheep that has gotten low. To get a sheep back up on their feet, the shepherd will have to exercise both persistence and vigilance. It can be done, but in the process there is so much pain, so much loss that is entirely unnecessary. If only the sheep could have remained healthy and avoided all this needless suffering! This concept gives us the correct perspective on the great need to maintain a healthy flock.

Hoof Care. One aspect of a sheep's health should be a major concern for the shepherd, and that is the care of their hooves. It is not only important for the individual sheep, but for the entire flock that their hooves remain in good condition. This simple maintenance can save a shepherd a lot of extra work.

Sheep must periodically have their hooves trimmed. This is not optional. It is absolutely crucial to their health. As a sheep walks around in the field, its hooves pick up particles that contain germs. These germs can become embedded in any cut or crevice in the hoof. Over time, an infection can set up, and the sheep will become lame. If this happens, the shepherd will notice a sheep hopping on three legs, or lagging behind due to a limp.

The shepherd attempts to prevent this problem by trimming their hooves. This should be done at least three times per year, as well as on an individual basis when necessary. Now, there is nothing pleasant about this process. It is hard on the sheep, and it is hard on the shepherd. This is not done for enjoyment, but for health. It is simply one of those things that we must do, regardless of whether or not we enjoy it.

The shepherd will take the sheep and sit it up on its rump, leaning it back against his legs. This will give the sheep a comical, undignified appearance that will place it completely at the mercy of the shepherd. All four hooves will now be accessible to the shepherd's care. The shepherd will begin by taking a hoof and inspecting its outer growth. The more outer growth on the hoof, the more debris it will carry. He will take his blade, and much like trimming fingernails, he will trim off the excess up to the pad of the hoof. This makes everything even and smooth. He will then inspect between the hooves to see if there is anything hidden. If so, he will take his blade and rake it between the hooves to clear away whatever might be there.

Walking through the field guarantees contamination. It is impossible to avoid this. When you consider this truth with a spiritual application, the field is clearly the world.

The field is the world; the good seed are the children of the kingdom; but the tares are the children of the wicked <one>; (Matthew 13:38)

The Lord understands where we are. He is aware of our surroundings. In John chapter seventeen the Lord spends some time talking to the Father. In this discourse, He begins to pray for His disciples. We notice, first of all, that the Lord points out their location:

And now I am no more in the world, but these are in the world, and I come to thee. Holy Father, keep through thine own name those whom

thou hast given me, that they may be one, as we
<are>. (John 17:11)

He acknowledges the fact that the disciples are going to be left *in the world* as He is preparing to leave by the way of the cross. Isn't it just like Him to be concerned for those that follow Him, instead of being concerned for Himself? What a wonderful Shepherd we have!

He then points out that, although the disciples will be left *in the world*, they are not *of the world*.

They are not of the world, even as I am not
of the world. (John 17:16)

This gives us a separating line between the Lord's disciples and the world. There is a difference here. We may be *in* this place, but we are not *of* this place. This world is not what we are about. It's not who we are. We are pilgrims passing through a hostile land. Passing through brings contamination and the Lord is aware of this. Notice the next verse:

Sanctify them through thy truth: thy word is
truth. As thou hast sent me into the world, even so
have I also sent them into the world. And for their

sakes I sanctify myself, that they also might be sanctified through the truth. (John 17:17-19)

To sanctify means to purify, to cleanse, to remove anything that would defile you. To be sanctified is to be made holy. And how does He say to do this? "Through thy word; thy word is truth." He tells the Father to sanctify us through His word.

So we can see that the field is the world, and since we are in the world, we become contaminated by the world. However, we also see the prayer of our Lord. "Sanctify them through thy word." He takes the blade of His Word and trims our hooves. He inspects us to see if anything has become hidden from plain view to prevent a future infection, and it is not pleasant to the sheep. As we sit in the house of God, the Word of God begins to trim away our excess and inspect us for all foreign materials. We become vulnerable. We may even begin to look and feel foolish, but *this is for our good.* It's a necessary thing, absolutely crucial to our health. As the shepherd begins to remove the foreign objects from our lives, we experience relief. Those things that we accidentally pick up irritate us, even cause us pain. As we carry them, we are convinced it's no big deal. But when they're removed, such a weight is lifted! Such freedom is experienced, such liberty is given, and the shepherd knows this. Let us not balk and struggle against this necessary process: it is for our health! May we learn to appreciate a Shepherd that is willing and able to do the unpleasant things that we need in order to assure us of health and happiness.

Foot Rot. This condition occurs when a sheep walks through a contaminated area after receiving an injury in its hoof. An infection sets up, and the hoof literally begins to rot. To a shepherd, foot rot is clearly identified by the scent that comes from the infected hoof. There is nothing quite like it. It often begins as nothing more than a small cut, but if left unattended, the sheep will become so sick with infection that death may occur.

The parallel can be easily identified in the life of a Christian. This typifies the damage that is done when a believer is wounded and then proceeds to walk through the fields of the world. That is when the contamination of this world no longer remains on the outside, but it works its way *within*. This sets up a spiritual infection. With it, it brings fever, weakness, and poison. The infected Christian begins the slow process of decline. It starts with a lack of appetite and a limp in their walk. The infection then spreads to the other feet as the sheep walks in its own contamination. Before long, it loses its ability to even *stand*. That's when more external contaminants move in, such as flies that lay eggs on these places, and the situation becomes much worse.

If a sheep gets to this point, there is no quick and simple cure. The shepherd must take extensive measures to rid the sheep of this rot.

First, he must be able to handle the sheep. I have seen sheep that had such a bad case of foot rot that they couldn't even walk to the watering trough. And yet, when I would approach them to help, they would use all of their strength to get up and flee. Isn't it amazing how Christians do the same thing to our loving Shepherd? Even when we have damaged ourselves and are in need of His help, we still resist His care! I often wonder how bad a person must get before they realize that their way is not working. A sheep, or a Christian, in this state is only making their life worse.

Secondly, the shepherd must *cut away* all of the rot. This is a difficult process for both the shepherd and the sheep. He must take his trimmers and cut down into the hoof until he gets to the living tissue. All of the rot must be removed in order for the healthy part to heal. This will cause the hoof to be uneven and damaged for a time. Make no mistake about it: the sheep will experience pain during this surgery, but it is a necessary pain.

Thirdly, after the rot and filth has been cleaned away, the exposed tissue must be coated with a balm. This balm will immediately bring some comfort to the sheep. The pain of this experience will turn to a sweet time of relief, just as The Comforter brings peace to us in times of great distress.

Finally, the sheep will be placed in a stall where it is easily accessible to the shepherd. There will be a time of closeness and care as the shepherd continues to care for the injured sheep.

Can you see the picture here, Christian? Can't you see the wounded child of God that turns to the world in spite and in bitterness? These wounds can come from anywhere, even church. Quite often it does! People turn to the ungodly, filthy places of the world for their solace, and then the wound becomes infected even worse due the contribution of the new contamination that they have introduced in their weakened state. This process often continues until the Christian becomes lame, damaged, and weak in their suffering. If this is where you are, I will not lie to you friend: the way back is not an easy one, but it is *needful*. The shepherd is the only cure! If you will bow to Him, then He will begin to cut away all of the contaminate in your mind and soul. Only Jesus can remove all of the bitterness, jealousy, hate, strife, and contention that has festered in your heart. This is an unpleasant ordeal, but isn't it always difficult when our shepherd causes us to look upon our sins? Don't let fear keep you from the Shepherd! While there must be some pain in cutting away the rot, there is great relief in the application of the balm: it takes the pain away! This is a comfort that only comes from the Lord, it is an inner peace that cannot be explained on paper. I believe the Apostle Paul had it right when he said:

And the peace of God, which passeth all understanding, shall keep your hearts and minds through Christ Jesus. (Philippians 4:7)

Please understand: *now* is the time of healing. The hoof is damaged. Parts of the sheep have been lost due to the infection. The shepherd has cut away all of the lost parts and discarded them. This sheep is not going to be in any condition to return to the field for some time. It must remain in close proximity to the shepherd while the damaged parts grow back. Eventually it will become whole again, but not right away. It is a mistake to send a wounded Christian that has come back to the Lord out into the field of service right away: they are not ready! They are not whole! Take the burden of service off of them, and give them time to heal. Encourage them to sit in church and listen to the word of God. Tell them to pray and experience closeness with their Shepherd as the Comforter continues to apply healing to their hurt. This time of separation from the flock is beneficial to all. It benefits the wounded sheep in its ease of burden and responsibility, which gives it time to focus on healing. It gives the flock time to regain confidence in the wounded sheep and to be assured that it is not spreading contaminant to the others. It gives the Shepherd time to draw closer to the wounded sheep, for He desires to be close to His sheep.

I am confident that there are some reading this who have been wounded. Perhaps you have turned to the world for your solace, and now you're sick with the rot of sin and the flesh. Make your way back to the Shepherd! It is fearful, it is scary, but it is your only hope of healing. Allow him to cut away all of the poison, to deal with that which is killing you. Only then will you experience His comfort and healing.

I feel that it is necessary to specify that passage is written concerning the flock. These are the sheep in our churches. But what about the under-shepherds that experience the wounds of battle? There is a separation that must be understood concerning these men. They are not the sheep, and thus this application is not for them. To suffer the wounds of battle is a part of the job. Just as our shepherd suffered for us, so must we suffer for our flocks! Many times there is pain and discomfort involved. There is betrayal, disappointment, concern, discouragement, anger, sorrow, and many more emotional experiences that leave their mark on the pastor. What should we do? As far as I can tell, our remedy is plain:

Humble yourselves therefore under the mighty hand of God, that he may exalt you in due time: Casting all your care upon him; for he careth for you.

Be sober, be vigilant; because your adversary the devil, as a roaring lion, walketh about, seeking whom he may devour: Whom resist stedfast in the faith, knowing that the same afflictions are accomplished in your brethren that are in the world. (1 Peter 5:6-9)

Brethren, let us be sober, vigilant, and strong. Let us take our wounds before our Shepherd who suffered for us. Let us not be weary in well doing. Be strong, quit you like men, stand fast. We must simply continue to contend for the faith. He will heal our wounds! He will supply our needs! He will see us through!

Pasture Rotation.

It is important for a shepherd to continually move his sheep from one pasture to another. A sheep that stays in the same pasture for too long, eating over the same places, will be a sickly sheep that will eventually die. Although some of this truth has already been considered under the instinct to pasture, there are other applications that are important for us to see as His sheep.

Sheep are called "the living lawnmowers" due to their ability to eat grass down to the dirt. If a flock of sheep are left on a pasture to long, they can literally kill the grass off completely by pulling it up by the roots. The application for us as His sheep is one of profound truth. If a congregation remains in the same place for to long, the pasture will die. This is seen in the numerous churches that have stayed the same for years and years. Slowly the congregation has grown old and no youth come in. The same messages have been preached, the same testimonies have been given over and over to the point that the flock has nothing good to eat, and the pasture dies. It is due to this that the Good Shepherd will lead his flock from one pasture to another. He will give us a time in the tablelands, then He will give us a time in the valley. This rotation between the pastures gives the sheep a fresh field to enjoy, and the sheep need freshness in their life. A church that is always shouting will grow numb to the rejoicing of the saints. A church that is always in the valley will become depressed and discouraged. We need to face the trials, and we need to experience the victories. Pastors do not need to avoid these transitions: they need to recognize the field that the Good Shepherd is leading them through and call the flock to follow.

<u>Internal Parasites.</u>

There is further danger to consider in this scenario. When sheep remain on one pasture for too long, the grass and the ground become infested with parasites. As the sheep continue to pick at the remainder of the grass and lick at the dirt, they ingest these parasites, and these parasites lay their eggs within the stomach or intestines of the sheep. This will then not only breed more parasites within the animal, but they will spread throughout the rest of the flock through the sheep's excrement.

This is a cycle that becomes very difficult to stop. Even if you move the flock, after the parasites have taken a host, parasites are incredibly resilient. It is for this reason that a good shepherd will keep his flock moving.

I have seen such spiritual parasites infect a congregation to the point of destruction. These vile contaminants, such as jealousy, bitterness, strife, and pride, will not only affect one member, but they will spread throughout the entire church. Once these parasites have taken root, they often lead to a major upheaval within the congregation, or even a church split. The only hope for such an infestation is to apply the remedy, and that is the preaching of the Word of God! Only by killing the parasites can the flock be delivered. In spite of all of the self-help books and philosophies that are offered to the public, these things cannot be destroyed through the will of men or the strength of the flesh. It is only through the power of the Scriptures that such things as pride can be dealt with. There is power in the Word that you will find nowhere else, and the preaching of the word, seasoned by the Holy Spirit, is the remedy to these parasites!

However, a flock that has been left to these parasitic infested fields for too long will most likely suffer loss. There will be some that are too far gone, and the application of the remedy will have a negative effect. They will resist the medicine. Speaking of a literal flock, I have had some die in spite of all of the aggressive medical attention that they were given. This also happens in a church that faces such a thing. When the Word is finally preached, some will be so far gone that *they will not be able to endure sound doctrine*. These will forsake the flock. They will not be able to allow the Word of God to eradicate the infestation within! This is sad, but a truth nonetheless.

There is another scenario that is played out under these circumstances that perhaps cannot be seen in comparison to a real flock of sheep, due to the fact that they are just sheep, and they cannot seek out their own pasture. In many cases where the under-shepherd allows the church to remain too long in one pasture, those who desire to grow will *leave*. They will seek out a different under-shepherd, fresh pasture, and a healthy environment. I am not writing this to advise church members to leave their church: I am writing this to help pastors to prevent this from happening in their flock. Preventive maintenance is the best medicine for this situation. The infestation of such spiritual parasites that are found in the hearts of men *always* lead to the destruction of the flock! Those who are carriers of these pests will spread them amongst their brethren. Those who desire a healthy atmosphere will leave to find fresh pasture.

We can see the importance of preventive maintenance. It is crucial to keep the sheep growing on fresh, clean pasture. An under-shepherd (pastor) who does not consistently lead his flock into fresh pastures in the word of God will fail to deal with the internal parasites that will set up within his people. The health of the congregation is very dependent upon this truth. If they are to be a happy, thankful flock, then they must be led into fresh pasture.

So we thy people and sheep of thy pasture will give thee thanks for ever: we will show forth thy praise to all generations. (Psalms 79:13)

External Parasites.

While this problem is not nearly as serious as internal parasites, it can still lower production in a sheep and, if left unchecked, the entire flock. Due to the wool of a sheep, there is an ongoing battle against external parasites. However, as with our previous discussions, proper maintenance can prevent serious problems.

Ticks, mites, and flies are such external parasites that can plague a flock of sheep to the point of preventing their rest. Sheep need to be able to lie down in safety and peace. This is their time for chewing the cud and producing both milk for their lambs and wool to be sold. An infested flock will exhibit poor wool and a loss of weight. Their milk production will drop and, if feeding twin lambs, this can be disastrous. The shepherd must keep a constant, watchful eye on his flock to prevent such things, as well as a scheduled application of some type of parasite control.

To gain an even better understanding of this problem, let us consider the nature of a parasite. These filthy things survive off of the life of their host. They are blood suckers that slowly drain the very life from the poor creature that they inhabit. Thus, every shepherd should hate these parasites, as should the sheep. When we consider the external parasites, these things that tag themselves to the outside of the flesh, many things come to mind. And just as the internal parasites that drain our life can be seen in such things as pride, jealousy, strife, and bitterness, so can external parasites be seen in such things as pornography, drunkenness, riotous living, ungodly acquaintances that influence our decisions, a job that keeps us out of church, and so forth. These things that attach themselves to our lives and our flesh will, if left unchecked, slowly drain away our strength, change our focus, and severely hinder our production.

Of course, as in all sheep care, the best medicine is *prevention*. Just as this is true of an actual flock, so is it true of a church. The prevention of external parasites is never easy. It is work, plain and simple. It involves effort, determination, perseverance, and consistency on the part of the Shepherd, and on the part of the sheep, it involves submission to the care of the Shepherd and His under-shepherd.

The solution for this problem is not so much the rotation of the flock as it is the personal, individual care of the Shepherd. Periodically, it is absolutely crucial for the shepherd to *lay his hands on each individual sheep*. This is particularly true in shearing season. In fact, shearing season is the primary prevention for external parasites. A sheep's wool becomes infused with everything it touches, and many parasites will try to set up down next to the skin. Throughout the year, the shepherd often finds it necessary to cut off the "tags" that build up on a sheep. These tags will collect manure and parasites that can damage the animal. So the shepherd must catch the sheep, handle the sheep, and remove these things that have tagged on to it. It's never pleasant, nor desired by either the sheep or its shepherd, but without it, the sheep will suffer.

This typically occurs whenever shearing season comes around, and it is hard work for all involved. Each year, I would set up with my shearers, some sort of antiseptic, and my hoof trimmers, and the work would begin. I would typically look around to find the sheep that I felt was in the worst shape to begin. It has always been my experience that the worst sheep is the one that was, by nature, the most resistant to the leadership of the shepherd. This is the sheep that is always going where it shouldn't go, sticking its head where it shouldn't, and thus it has the filthiest wool of them all. I would catch this sheep and immediately experience pain in my hands due to the thorns and cockleburs... the filthiness of this sheep would hurt the shepherd! I would then take hold of its front legs, lift it up, and sit it on its rump, leaning it back against my knees. The condition of this sheep's underbelly would be horribly matted. I would take the shearers, place the blade against the skin at the brisket area, and begin pushing the blades in a downward motion.

Now, it must be understood that our wool is our *works*, and the places we go and the things we do determine what is in our wool. A sheep that has remained in the barn or field where the shepherd left them would be finished in a short time, because the blade of the shearers would have room between the skin and the outer layer of wool to cut. But the sheep that has been in places it should *not* be will have gotten the filth down to the skin. This is where the external parasites set up. The shearers will have to be forced through the debris and filth in order to remove it. Often this has grown to the skin, and the shearers will cut the sheep. This extra process is both time-consuming and difficult. The sheep experiences pain and must be handled roughly to remove such things, but to ignore it is to doom the sheep.

Please understand that I do not believe the under-shepherd should be a brow beater, or even a sheep beater. But I do know that there are times when the flock must be sheared. I am speaking of a cleaning, a removing of the tags, or even a complete removal of the worldly affect that is upon us. Sometimes it becomes necessary for the under-shepherd to take the Word of God and begin cutting away such things.If you are a sheep in need of such, then you will experience the handling of the Lord. He, not the under-shepherd, but the *Good Shepherd* will begin to work on you and work *in* you to remove the things that are damaging your production. This is the need of the shearing.

CHAPTER THREE

LAMBING

Lambing time is a very special time for a shepherd. There is a sense of accomplishment and victory over every healthy birth and every successful bonding between a ewe and her lamb. The entire process brings a shepherd and the individual sheep closer together. These moments of closeness during the process of birthing are very reflective of the relationship between Christ and His believers.

Flushing.

"Flushing" refers to the practice of increasing the protein intake of the flock in order to cause an increase in fertility. When the shepherd decides it is near the time to put the ram in with the ewes, he will first begin to give them either more sweet feed or a better feed with higher protein. This will cause the ewes to conceive more easily, and often it will even cause them to give birth to twins. The increase of their protein actually increases their fertility.

On the flip side, a poor sheep that is not properly fed will *not* be fertile. Even if they do conceive, most of the time they will lose the lamb. Proper nutrition is a *must* when it comes to the health of a mother ewe and her lamb.

As pastors and under-shepherds, we cannot take this point seriously enough. Our flocks absolutely *must* be properly fed! The great necessity for spiritual nutrition is present throughout the scriptures:

Take heed therefore unto yourselves, and to all the flock, over the which the Holy Ghost hath made you overseers, to feed the church of God, which he hath purchased with his own blood. (Acts 20:28)

Could that be stated any clearer? Paul even goes further still to explain why it was so important that the church of God be fed:

For I know this, that after my departing shall grievous wolves enter in among you, not sparing the flock. (Acts 20:29)

He knew that they were going to need both strength and stability. These can only come through a proper diet of the Word of God. They need to be fed! This truth is further taught in the Epistle of Peter:

The elders which are among you I exhort, who am also an elder, and a witness of the sufferings of Christ, and also a partaker of the glory that shall be revealed: Feed the flock of God which is among you, taking the oversight <thereof>, not by constraint, but willingly; not for filthy lucre, but of a ready mind; Neither as being lords over <God's> heritage, but being ensamples to the flock. And when the chief Shepherd shall appear, ye shall receive a crown of glory that fadeth not away. (1 Peter 5:1-4)

While proper nutritional care is something that the flock needs at all times, "flushing" is not a continual process, but rather a seasonal one. With my own flock, I learned that they were short-day breeders. That is to say that my ewes would often breed when the days began to get shorter and the temperature cooler. It was at the onset of these shorter, cooler days when I would begin to flush their feed.

As, under-shepherds it is crucial for us to know the proper season of our spiritual flock. In knowing this, we understand that there is a time when our congregation is in need of a stronger nutrition. In many cases, we practice this without even realizing it. When a church begins to plan a big evangelistic push, such as a "big day" or "family day," we pastors will often take several services prior to the event to preach messages rich in evangelism. That is a prime example of flushing the feed of our flock: it is adding an increase in the proper nutrition needed for the season of new births!

Production.

Shepherds love their sheep. That is a fact. However, it needs to be understood that the shepherd intends for each one of his sheep to be productive. The sheep that does not contribute to the production of the flock will receive special attention and medicine in an attempt to correct whatever deficiency it has. Furthermore, the shepherd of a literal flock will cull, or separate, those sheep who are a drain on the production of others and replace them with ewes who are a benefit.

Of course, the relationship of the Good Shepherd and His sheep is much more forgiving and longsuffering than a literal shepherd, but the principle still stands; there is no doubt that the Good Shepherd desires for His sheep to be productive.

But the fruit of the Spirit is love, joy, peace, longsuffering, gentleness, goodness, faith, Meekness, temperance: against such there is no law. (Galatians 5:22-23)

Herein is my Father glorified, that ye bear much fruit; so shall ye be my disciples. (John 15:8)

Although the Lord is both longsuffering and forgiving, He is also very wise when it comes to production of His flock. He is not willing to sacrifice the productivity of His entire flock for one sheep that is not submissive to His leadership. There have been many circumstances when the Lord has found it necessary to cull one of His in order to protect the health and productivity of the flock. This is always unfortunate and regretful, but it does happen. It would behoove us as Christians to faithfully follow our Shepherd!

One might ask, why take such a drastic measure? Why would the shepherd find it necessary to literally remove a sheep from the flock, just because it may be hindering production? The answer is in the product itself. The main product of a flock is not wool. The returns on wool are very minimal in comparison to the cost of the provisions for the flock. The main product of a flock is its *lambs*. A sheep that hinders the production of the lambs is hurting the growth of the flock. I have had sheep that spent all of their time walking around and butting into the other ewes just to establish themselves as the head of the butting order. As you can imagine, this kept the flock in a state of constant irritation. I remember one particular ewe that walked up to another ewe, who was lying down at the time, and proceeded to butt into her till she gave up her spot. The offending ewe then lay down in that spot just long enough for the first ewe to find another place to lie, and then that butting ewe proceeded to repeat the process over again. This would become such a problem that the flock could not rest! A shepherd cannot allow this behavior to continue, for a lack of rest can cause serious issues in the flock. In particular, this can cause problems for the unborn lambs and even affect the ability of the ewes to conceive. Sometimes it is necessary to take drastic measures in order to prevent such issues from taking hold. The peace and unity of the flock are vital when it comes to the birthing of lambs.

A ewe will carry her lamb for a period of one hundred and forty-two (142) to one hundred and fifty-two (152) days, or approximately five months. Of course, we know that five is the number of grace. So we can see the connection here, that the birth of a lamb is accomplished through grace. However, during the period of gestation (the time of carrying the lamb from conception to delivery) there are issues that can hinder the birth and even cause the lamb to become aborted. Unrest is absolutely one of these issues. The temperament of a ewe that is heavy with lamb is delicate at its best. During this period, I would attempt to make the ewes as comfortable as possible. I would make sure that they were kept in a place with plenty of room to move around, with sufficient feed for their needs, and water that was easily accessible. Most of the time there would be no problem until one of the flock became irritated. This would usually occur between two, sometimes three ewes who would face-off and begin butting heads. I recall multiple occasions when it became necessary for me to intervene, separating the ewes until the conflict had receded. In spite of the fact that the health of their lambs was at stake, they were too involved with their own issues to see the danger at hand.

The illustration here should be simple and clear to the believer. How often have we seen brothers or sisters square-off and begin butting heads over some silly slight, never realizing the damage that they had caused to the expected new births? We've seen parents who would actually leave the church over an arbitrary statement that someone made, only to quit church altogether with lost children in the home. Please allow me to exhort you to make the birth of these unborn lambs a top priority in your lives! Do not allow something so minuscule and unimportant to hinder their birth!

The production of the flock is accomplished by the sheep, not the shepherd. It may be a simple truth, but a truth nonetheless. Sheep bear sheep. It is the watch-care and provision of the shepherd that gives them what they need in order to produce lambs and wool, but it is the sheep themselves who do the actual birthing. This responsibility should weigh heavily upon us as we accept this truth. Each individual member of the congregation should bear the burden of the unborn. Each member should bear a desire to see new births with great anticipation. Oh, how I recall witnessing the joy of the saints, when as a young boy I saw sinners walk the aisle and receive Christ! Their tears flowed, their shouts rang, and the brethren embraced one another in celebration. News of the new convert would spread throughout the community. Why, before the next service, people all around would have heard of the sinner that was saved, that new birth that had occurred… It is an unfortunate truth that the church doesn't seem nearly as concerned or excited about new births as they were in those days long passed. The zeal of the church has lessened over the repentance of a sinner. Our desire to see them born does not *weigh* on us as it once did, and as it still should. Lord, please rekindle the fiery burden for sinners in the hearts of your sheep!

Birthing.

Once breeding season had passed, it wouldn't be long at all before the shepherd could tell if a ewe was carrying a lamb. Most of them would begin to show in a short amount of time, especially if they were carrying multiple lambs. So the shepherd would keep his eyes on the flock, watching for signs of birth in each of the ewes. He knows them individually, after all. He knows their strengths, he knows their weaknesses, and he knows their needs. He knows which ones are experienced, which ones aren't, and how to assist each one in birth.

As the ewe grows closer to birthing, the burden gets heavy. I have been in the barn with the flock as they were all lying down, chewing, and you could hear a ewe groaning as the time of the birth was drawing near. I would make my way through them without disturbing their calm to locate the mother who was under the load. I would lay my hands on her, checking her progress, and then easily move her to a place of solitude. When the ewe gets to this point, she is not sociable. She is not interested in mingling. She wants to be alone with her shepherd, and she wants to see the birth of the lamb. This is a good place to be.

I have never been one to believe that the church should primarily be a place of solemnity, but rather a place of joy, laughter, happiness and unity. That being said, I also believe that the burden for the lost should cause us to have a sincerity and sobriety in our worship. We might feel free to laugh, but we are not flippant. We may enjoy a light-spirited service, but we also recognize the seriousness of the hour. I have clearly recognized a loss of the burden for sinners in our congregations. We need our tears to return for the unborn! Every so often, it would be a great encouragement to see a member of the flock standing off from the crowd, not because they are offended, nor due to some particular person they don't like, but because their heavy burden has brought a desire to be alone with the Shepherd. They bear a great weight, and they feel the pressure of it. In such a case, they need the attention of their Shepherd.

The birth of a lamb is accomplished with the shepherd looking on. Generally, I would stand to the side and observe, allowing the natural process that our creator instituted to occur. Unless there was a complication, everything would proceed through its natural course. The lamb would experience its first stimulant in this world as it felt the nose of its mother and hear the gluttering sounds that she would make. The temperature was usually cold at this time of year, so it was very important that the lamb receive what is known as the "first-milk" from its mother within thirty minutes of its birth. The shepherd knows this. If the lamb does not get this first-milk, then it will become chilled and die. And so the shepherd watches as the lamb finds its legs and stands after several attempts. The mother ewe will then walk around the lamb to position herself so the lamb's nose is directed toward her udders. She would then nudge the lamb toward this life-giving substance. The lamb would take its nose and literally thrust its head into its mother in order to find the milk.

I've witnessed this event on multiple occasions. Honestly, it is a miracle to see a creature that has just come into the world seeming to know exactly what to do. As the lamb got its first taste of this milk, it would show great enthusiasm. Its tail would begin to move energetically, and it would put more effort into gaining more of this milk. Once I had seen this process completed, I knew that the lamb would be alright. The cold would not get it. The environment would not kill it. It had the first milk within it now. It will be strong.

Colostrum.

This first milk, or colostrum, contains antibodies and nutrients that cannot be found anywhere else. Oh, there are substitutes out there, and even homemade remedies that are supposed to take its place if a shepherd needs to bottle feed a newborn, but I have never had any real success with these. There is just no substitute for the first milk of the ewe. There is also no substitute for the milk of the Word in the life a new convert.

Now, I need to specify my view here concerning the relationship between the mother ewe and the lamb and the significance of the first milk, followed by the mother's milk.

As I previously stated, the first-milk, or colostrum, is what the lamb gets immediately after birth. This milk is a temporary fix for the lamb. It does not last long, but the small amount that the lamb receives is enough to fortify and strengthen it to begin development. In my view, this first-milk represents the extra provision of the Holy Spirit for a new convert. In this analogy, the position of the mother ewe is fulfilled by the Holy Spirit. To be clear, I do not view the church as a mother of new converts: the church is not a mother, but a chaste virgin of Christ.

For I am jealous over you with godly jealousy: for I have espoused you to one husband, that I may present <you as> a chaste virgin to Christ. (2 Corinthians 11:2)

Further evidence of this is present in the fact
that we are not born through the church, as the catholics
suggest, but rather we are born of the Spirit:

**Jesus answered, Verily, verily, I say unto
thee, Except a man be born of water and <of> the
Spirit, he cannot enter into the kingdom of God. That
which is born of the flesh is flesh; and that which is
born of the Spirit is spirit. Marvel not that I said unto
thee, Ye must be born again. The wind bloweth
where it listeth, and thou hearest the sound thereof,
but canst not tell whence it cometh, and whither it
goeth: so is every one that is born of the Spirit.
(John 3:5-8)**

This passage makes it clear that life-giving
nourishment for the newborn is supplied by the sweet
presence of the Holy Spirit. He gives the lamb, the
newborn convert, the extra nourishment that it needs to
strengthen its legs and fortify its immunity.

After the colostrum, or first-milk, is depleted, it is
then replaced with the mother's milk. Again, we
understand that the Holy Spirit is the mother in this case,
and the mother's milk is the milk of the Word that is

revealed to the newborn *by* the Holy Spirit. There is absolutely *no substitute* for the milk of the Word in the life of a new convert!

Wherefore laying aside all malice, and all guile, and hypocrisies, and envies, and all evil speakings, As newborn babes, desire the sincere milk of the word, that ye may grow thereby: If so be ye have tasted that the Lord <is> gracious. (1 Peter 2:1-3)

In the first verse from this passage, you can see the danger for the newborn: malice, guile, hypocrisy, envy, and evil speaking. This is the sort of cold environment that can take the very life of a newborn. It is important that the under-shepherd protects them from the depravity of a world that wants to destroy them.

Now notice the second verse and see how that the newborn desires the sincere milk of the Word. If they taste it, they will want it. This sincere milk is delicious to the newborn. Also, notice how it says "that ye may grow *thereby*." That is to say, a newborn grows by the power of the milk of the Word!

Finally, notice the third verse, which defines what exactly the "milk of the Word" really is. "If so be ye have tasted that the Lord is gracious." The milk of the Word is the story and account of the Lord Jesus Christ. These newly-born converts need to learn about the Lord, to fall in love with Him, and to grow thereby. For this reason, I have always been a strong advocate of the Sunday School program in the local church. From infancy to adulthood, our churches must provide classes that will take a person from the basics of the bible to the complexities of the scriptures: here a little, and there a little. Newborn Christians *desperately* need to be fed the first-milk of the Word of God, so that they will be protected from the dangers of their surrounding environment.

Substitutes.

There are many substitutes out there for both the first-milk and the mother's milk. Some are available through suppliers, while others are homemade.

For colostrum, I have tried both types of substitute. I created home remedies by mixing many different ingredients: raw eggs for protein, syrup for energy, and vitamins for fortification. Of course, substitutes found on store shelves are pre-mixed and ready for use. I can honestly say that, in my experience, neither substitute was successful. They might have kept the lamb alive, but it never prospered.

As we have already stated, this is a picture of the Word of God that is tasted when a new convert learns about the Lord. In the literal flock, colostrum is not only needful and helpful, but it is absolutely necessary to life for the newborn. Without this first-milk, the lamb will die. I firmly believe that there is no substitute invented by man that a shepherd can successfully use to replace it. While I am speaking of a physical shepherd in this statement, I also believe that this applies to the spiritual flock. *There is no substitute for our bible*! While this might be a statement pointed at the many different "versions" of our bible that are offered today, it is more than that. I will state that our King James, 1611 Bible is the Word of God preserved for the English speaking people, and there is no substitute. However, I would also like to state that it is equally destructive to attempt to replace the milk of the Word with other things. Many churches are trying to keep their young ones by offering exciting youth activities and entertainment. They have pulled them out of the services and placed them in chatting sessions rather than allowing them to feast on the scriptures... This will not work. They must have the milk of the Word! I am not trying to say that they *need* the milk of the Word: I am saying that they will *die* without it! They will not last, they will not grow, they will not develop. *They must learn of Him*, or else they will become heavy-laden and faint!

Come unto me, all <ye> that labour and are heavy laden, and I will give you rest. Take my yoke upon you, and learn of me; for I am meek and lowly in heart: and ye shall find rest unto your souls. For my yoke <is> easy, and my burden is light. (Matthew 11:28-30)

He said "learn of me." Amen, learn of Him! Only by learning of Him can a newborn become identified with

Him! In understanding the importance of this step, we can see the beautiful picture of the believer.

Grafting.

The colostrum gives the lamb the scent of its mother. This becomes essential in having a successful lambing year due to the loss of lambs and complications of ewes. Often a lamb would be still-born or experience birthing complications that would cause it to die. This would leave a ewe without a lamb to care for. In another stall, a ewe would give birth to three lambs, but only produce enough milk for two. When this would happen, I would take the deceased lamb, skin it, and place its pelt on one of the three from the neighboring stall, much like putting on a coat. I would then place this lamb in the stall with the ewe who had lost her lamb. At first, she would believe that it was hers due to her scent on the lamb's new coat. But in order for her to *continue* to accept it, the lamb *must* ingest the ewe's first-milk. This would often take a few days to accomplish, and as these days would pass, the pelt would dry out, changing the scent.

However, by the time it would become necessary to remove the pelt, the lamb would have eaten the mother's first-milk. With that colostrum running through its entire system, it would literally cause the lamb to have the specific scent of its new mother. With sheep, this process is called **grafting**.

What a beautiful picture of a sinner becoming a saint! We see the sinner realizing that the milk of the world is insufficient to meet their needs, and then that same sinner hears the gospel message,and puts their faith in Christ, thereby having "put on" Christ. This principle is outlined in the book of Galatians.

First, it is initiated by faith.

For ye are all the children of God by faith in Christ Jesus. (Galatians 3:26)

Secondly, it is commenced by the baptism of the Holy Spirit. This is being baptized *into* Christ, and then we have *put on* Christ. That is the application of the slain lamb.

For as many of you as have been baptized into Christ have put on Christ. (Galatians 3:27)

Once we have put on Christ in the baptism of the Holy Spirit, we are thereby *accepted in Christ*. It matters not if you are a Jew or Greek, bond or free. You are now accepted as a child of God!

There is neither Jew nor Greek, there is neither bond nor free, there is neither male nor female: for ye are all one in Christ Jesus. And if ye <be> Christ's, then are ye Abraham's seed, and heirs according to the promise. (Galatians 3:28-29)

Once we have the slain lamb put upon us, we become accepted. And as we ingest the milk of the Word, we become acclimated to the Christian faith.

Complications.

There are always complications with a flock of sheep when it comes to the birthing season. Some of these can be avoided by preventive maintenance, while other complications are beyond the control of the shepherd. Of course, I am speaking of the literal, earthly shepherd with a literal, earthly flock. Still, even in the spiritual realm, we are all free moral agents, and as much as our great Shepherd desires for lambs to be born into the fold, He does not supernaturally force people to be saved. He does, however, beckon mankind with a Shepherd's call: come unto me.

Preventive maintenance is *key* to a healthy birth. As I have already stated, an unborn lamb can be hurt or even killed by such things as the ewe getting butted by another sheep. A lack of nutrition can also cause the birth to be terminated, or the lamb could become deformed or paralyzed. Equally so, lambs can be lost when the flock is traumatized by some predator. The infection of both internal and external parasites can also complicate the pregnancy. Each of these factors should motivate a shepherd to practice consistent preventive maintenance. It is the shepherd's responsibility to keep his sheep well fed, healthy, and protected.

However, even if the shepherd follows each of these steps without fail, sometimes you lose lamb. Sometimes they are still-born or aborted by some unforeseen circumstances. It is important for a shepherd to recognize this truth. He must move on to the next possible birth. Don't let a loss tear you down: keep-on-keeping-on. As a pastor, I have also come to realize that there are times when you just *lose* one. It's heartbreaking. It *can* be devastating. But we must go on. There are times when you have exhausted every effort to win a sinner to Christ, and they still go on to leave this life without the Lord. Sometimes church members fall into the snares of the devil, and they leave the church. Whether it's a leader, a quiet member, an elder, or a youth, there are just going to be times when we *lose*.

I am thankful our Lord does not give up every time one walks away, and we know that His will is that all would come to Him.

The Lord is not slack concerning his promise, as some men count slackness; but is longsuffering to us-ward, not willing that any should perish, but that all should come to repentance. (2 Peter 3:9)

Even though He desires for all to come to repentance, we must realize that not all are saved. I assure you, there are those that the Lord has called who will not come to Him. Every day, more people leave this life without trusting Him as their Savior and Shepherd. He does not quit, He does not give up, and He does not despair. He reaches out to one after another. He is longsuffering, faithful and true! We as church leaders and church members must continue knocking on doors and sharing the gospel, even if we lose one! Keep in mind that not every youth is going to go to the world, not every husband is going to forsake his wife and children, and not every wife is going to follow a wolf into the world. As Christians, we often focus too much on our losses. What about all of the births that we have seen? What about the families He has rescued, the marriages He has healed, and the youths He has brought to Himself who have committed their life to Him?

> ***Finally, brethren, whatsoever things are true, whatsoever things \<are\> honest, whatsoever things \<are\> just, whatsoever things \<are\> pure, whatsoever things \<are\> lovely, whatsoever things \<are\> of good report; if \<there be\> any virtue, and if \<there be\> any praise, think on these things. (Philippians 4:8)***

Development.

At first, a newborn lamb is completely dependent on the milk of its mother for sustenance. The first-milk, as has been discussed, gives the lamb all that it needs to begin its life with a resistance to damaging bacteria and the like. However, the first-milk then becomes the simple milk of the mother, without the extra life-giving properties needed in its first few days of life. This mother's milk is sweet and greatly desired by the lamb. The lamb will continue to feed off its mother as long as it can, or as long as it is allowed to do so. Eventually the lamb is going to need to grow and develop, and to do that it must be weaned from the milk and transitioned to feed and roughage. This is necessary due to the digestive properties of a sheep. In order for a sheep to properly grow, it must gain the ability to ruminate, and that can only be done with a diet of roughage and feed. Even though the milk is sweet and sufficient at first, it cannot provide proper sustenance and nutrition in order for the lamb to develop into a healthy productive member of the flock.

This process of transition is brought about by three components. The first is the ewe itself. As the lamb grows, it becomes more aggressive in its feeding, not unlike a selfish, greedy person that cannot get enough of some vice. The lamb will become so aggressive that it will use its nose as a battering ram in an effort to cause more milk to come down at one time. This aggressive action will send the signal to the ewe that it's time to wean the lamb. Her first step in doing this will be to allow the lamb to get a little milk, then walk away after a moment of feeding. She will no longer stand still and allow the lamb to fill its greedy desire. However, this is often not enough to deter the lamb. If the lamb still persists, then the mother ewe will butt it aggressively. She will certainly not deal her child a damaging blow, but still one sharp enough to send a message, and that message is *no*. Our present-day society would condemn the ewe in this scenario. They would declare that the ewe was hampering the personal expression of the lamb. Perhaps this lamb doesn't want to develop into a member of the flock. Maybe this lamb wants to be something else. It's interesting, isn't it, that our present society doesn't consider the *love* that is shown each time the ewe butts the lamb? The effort of this ewe to wean her child is for its *development*. Without this step, the lamb will become sick and die. At best, it could live but become deformed and weak. It matters not what the lamb wants, nor does it matter what the lamb wants to be: it is a lamb, and it must be weaned in order to develop. I would also like to state that mankind's effort to reject what he is, how he is made, and what he needs in order to properly develop is equally ridiculous. Simply put, we must mature past the aggressive, greedy nature of a child and learn that there comes a time when we simply cannot have everything we want, when we want it.

The second component is the flock. The shepherd consistently provides sustenance for his sheep. If it is in the winter, he puts out good hay, which he keeps readily available at all times. He will also provide feed that he has developed to meet the nutritional needs of the flock. If it's in the spring or summer, he will move the flock from one pasture to another in a constant rotation. The sheep that have been under the shepherd for a significant amount of time will become accustomed to this and know when it is time to feed. The shepherd will come in and pour out the feed, or he'll call to the sheep to pass through into another pasture. Picture, if you will, a hungry lamb that is walking beside its mother. It goes under the ewe with its aggressive behavior and discovers that she will not let it get its fill. It then steps back, despondent, and sees its mother with her nose in a trough eating food from the shepherd. The lamb steps forward and puts its nose in the trough as well and takes its first bite of feed. Later, when out to pasture, the lamb will see its mother grazing on green grass. It will walk up and put its nose down right next to its mother's to taste what she is eating. What an example of God's children! How desperately do our young ones need to see those who have been under the shepherd for years feasting on the food that He has put out for us! They need to see us feasting on the meat of His Word, on the strength of our joy in Him, and on the fortitude that comes through a personal prayer life. They need to hear us speak of the victories of the Christian walk. Our young converts need to see a flock that enjoys the food of the pasture and the food of the trough. They need to see that a life lived for Christ is a *wonderful* life! If they can see the flock enjoying what God has provided, then they will step forward, put their nose to the ground, and taste for themselves:

O taste and see that the Lord <is> good: blessed <is> the man <that> trusteth in him. (Psalms 34:8)

The third component of development is the shepherd. He knows what a lamb needs in order to develop properly. Between the ewe and the shepherd, the lamb will have everything that they need for development. The shepherd brings the feed to the ewe, the ewe provides the milk to the lamb, and all of this is done in an area of safety and assurance. The atmosphere is peaceful, and there is no want or need within the stall. This total provision will continue until the time comes for the lamb to be weaned. The ewe will take the lamb through the process of weaning herself, but sometimes the lamb will resist. Although it might begin to eat from both the pasture and the trough, sometimes the lamb will continue to nurse for a while. I have witnessed a yearling go to its mother for milk and have to get on its knees, just to get to her milk. This is not good for the lamb, nor is it good for the ewe. When this happens, the shepherd will separate the lambs from their mothers for a period of time.

This separation always begins with a lot of noise. I remember those days, as I would go through the flock and take each lamb had nearly reached the size of their mothers, and I would put them in a separate-but-connected area within the barn. The lambs were still *with* their mothers, but they were no longer able to nurse. These lambs would bleat and cry like it was the end of the world. The cry of these younglings was, without question, overly dramatic. The only thing that they were being denied was the milk, not the mother! The mother was still there, the closeness was still provided, but it was time for the lambs to become ewes themselves.

The time was approaching for the mother ewes to be placed in with the ram for breeding, so they needed some time to gain in weight and strength. The lambs that would soon become replacements within the flock also needed to learn independence from their mothers so that they too could produce lambs. It was time for these lambs to experience all that it means to truly be a part of the shepherd's flock. They needed to know what it was like to have him come into the stall, put his hands on them, trim their hooves, check their wool, look at their teeth, provide their medicine, and provide them with food, minerals, and water. These lambs needed to realize that their sustenance does not come from the mother ewe, but rather it comes from the shepherd.

I fear that we have lost this concept in our churches. There comes a time when our young ones need to become productive members of the flock. They need to come to a place where their spiritual nourishment is no longer provided by those that have raised them, but from the Good Shepherd Himself! They must walk with Him themselves, rather than alongside their mothers and fathers. In doing so, they leave off from the pampered life of total provision and experience the joy of eating from their own labors. They themselves are fed due to their work in a Sunday School class, or from soul winning, or from a strong prayer life. In the area where I live, many of our churches are dying off because the young ones never matured in the flock. Eventually, they left and joined the world. This was due to their lack of development and discipleship in the flock.

Docking.

The term "docking" speaks of a process where the shepherd takes a device called a ring expander and places a small rubber band on the upper part of the lamb's tail. This ring will then cut off the blood supply to the tail, which will cause it to fall off. The band must be placed about an inch from the rump of the lamb, which leaves a small nub. This is not a comfortable experience for the lamb, but it's best to do this while it is young. I never performed this on a weak lamb. I would always wait until they got their feet under them, so that I could know that they were healthy and strong.

Immediately following the procedure, the lamb would ball up and usually fall over due to the discomfort of the band. I suppose this looked comical, something akin to watching a goat faint, but is was no picnic for the lamb. In spite of this discomfort, however, it was absolutely necessary for the well-being of the lamb. Due to the length of a sheep's tail, and the wool that would grow on it, the tail had to be removed or docked. If it wasn't, then the wool on the tail would become matted with manure from the sheep, and it would pick up whatever contaminants that were on the ground. This collection of filth on the tail becomes a breeding ground for external attack from things such as parasites, which brings a serious risk of death for the sheep.

Docking the tail is also needful for the purpose of breeding, which would help in the shepherd's production of the flock. As such, it is better to go ahead and remove this hindering part from its body while it is still young, rather than waiting until it has grown. Of course, this didn't happen all at once, but slowly. Once the band was placed, the undesired part would eventually fall off. After the first day of banding, the lamb would become used to the nagging discomfort and stop noticing it entirely. When the tail would finally fall off, the lamb wouldn't even know it. Such a small discomfort, inflicted by the shepherd, had separated the lamb from something that would later bring infection of the world and hindrance to its production.

It is equally necessary and needed for us to begin the process of mortification in the lives of our new converts while they are young. Oh not all at once for sure, but they need to become used to the process of restriction. The things in their lives that cling to the world, that hold to the disease of the flesh and that will re-contaminate them need to be removed. And it is much easier to remove these things while they are spiritually new and fresh. The tail of the sheep represents the old man, the old nature we are born with. It is that part of all mankind that desires to fulfill the lusts of the flesh, and this is something we are all born with.

Wherein in time past ye walked according to the course of this world, according to the prince of the power of the air, the spirit that now worketh in the children of disobedience: Among whom also we all had our conversation in times past in the lusts of our flesh, fulfilling the desires of the flesh and of the mind; and were by nature the children of wrath, even as others. (Ephesians 2:2-3)

Although the banding removes the vast majority of the tail, it can't be destroyed completely. As I stated, you place the band around an inch from the rump of the lamb, which leaves a nub remaining. This shows us that, although we can get rid of most of it, there will always be a little bit of that old nature that we're going to have to deal with until that day when we are finally redeemed from this body of flesh. Still, that little bit that remains is much more manageable than the entire tail.

I recall a certain sheep that I had purchased which had not had its tail removed... Its tail was a matted-up mess. I quickly realized that, if I did not get this issue remedied, then this sheep would have a consistent health problem. To band this sheep would have been both difficult and dangerous due to the size of its tail. This left me with one option: *amputation*. With a little help and a lot of study, I decided to remove its tail surgically. Suffice it to say that this process was *much* more painful and *much* more extensive than the banding of a newborn lamb. I feel the need to emphasize this point very clearly: **It is much harder to remove these things from our lives after we have gotten older!** In the realm of Christianity, when we do not begin the process of restriction while we are young, the things that hinder us become deeply embedded in our lives. That makes them extremely difficult to remove.

While they are young, we must show them the need for separation. We have to deal with their dress, their music, their language, their associations, their carnal appetites... They need to know the importance of removing these things from their lives. To this day, I have members who have become so attached to their worldly Christ-defying music that they cannot get any victory in their lives. **These adults will never have victory because they can't get free from the contamination!** However, if we will put restrictions on the old, carnal nature when they're young, just as the band restricts the flow of blood to the tail, then they will learn to deal with the restrictions while they're young. When they fall away, just as the tail does over time, they won't even feel their absence. Once those things are gone, the same ones that their flesh said they could not live without, they won't even miss them! The problem is, when we wait until adulthood to introduce restrictions, the process is always more difficult and more painful. If we will teach our children to resist their flesh *while they are young*, then their lives will be nothing but better for it.

CHAPTER FOUR

ALL ABOUT THE SHEPHERD

First and foremost, it is important for us to recognize and receive this crucial fact: the Lord Jesus is the Shepherd of the sheep. We know that this fact is indisputable by looking to the scriptures:

I am the good shepherd: the good shepherd giveth his life for the sheep. (John 10:11)

I am the good shepherd, and know my <sheep>, and am known of mine. (John 10:14)

My sheep hear my voice, and I know them, and they follow me: (John 10:27)

The sheep belong to the Shepherd. They are His, He owns them. It is all *His*: the flock, the production of the flock, the place where the flock abides, all of it.

Surely we can accept, as born-again believers, that the church is a flock of the Lord Jesus, and as such the church belongs to Him. The pulpit is His, the pews is

119

His, and all members who have truly accepted Christ are His. The work is His, and the ministry is His. The seed we sow is His seed, and the harvest we bring is His harvest. It is all to the glory of He who died for us! He is the shepherd of the sheep, and He is the shepherd of our very souls.

For ye were as sheep going astray; but are now returned unto the Shepherd and Bishop of your souls. (1 Peter 2:25)

It is vital that we recognize this point due to the tendency of humans to think that things belong to them. Too many preachers believe that it is *their* pulpit. Too many members use the term, "that is *my* church." No, friend, it is the Lord's. Not only is the building His, not only are the furnishings His, but so are the members within!

What? know ye not that your body is the temple of the Holy Ghost <which is> in you, which ye have of God, and ye are not your own? For ye are bought with a price: therefore glorify God in your body, and in your spirit, which are God's. (1 Corinthians 6:19-20)

What a profound phrase: "ye are not your own." I am familiar with that sheep who believed that it was its own master, that it belonged to no one but itself. Regardless of how it may have viewed the matter, it was wrong. In all honesty, it's humorous to consider a sheep that has the mentality that it is its own boss!

In all of my years combined as a shepherd, I suppose I must have owned more than one thousand sheep. Of course, this would include the flock that I kept and the crop of lambs that I would raise to sell. I can honestly say, in all of that time, I never owned *one*, not a single sheep, that I thought could care for itself. I know from personal experience that if any one of those sheep had gotten away from my protection, it would die. It would not be able to care for itself, it would not be able to feed itself, and it would not be able to protect itself. Now, how comical is it for one of these helpless creatures to think it belongs only to itself? After all, how was this foolish sheep going to shear itself? How was it going to trim its own hooves,so that it wouldn't contract foot rot and die of infection? Although it could find food for itself in the summer and fall months, what was it going to eat in the winter? It certainly could not cut, bale, and store hay for those harsh winter months. And just where would this sheep find shelter during the worst of the weather? The trees and the brush would not be adequate, and it wouldn't be able to build a barn itself.When the water froze, what would it drink? I believe that the point is very clear: how can something claim independence when it is completely depending on someone else for its basest of needs for survival?

Fret not that we are not our own! The glorious truth in this is, not only dows our Shepherd own us, but *He cares for us!* The Lord is *my* Shepherd, I shall not *want*! He is not an overlord, He is not a taskmaster: He is my Shepherd! How glad the sheep should be to submit themselves to His watch care! How willing and even *thankful* we should be to have such a Shepherd!

The under-shepherd and his Chief.

That being said, we also need to understand that our Shepherd has under-shepherds in His employ.

These under-shepherds are the pastors of our churches:

> *The elders which are among you I exhort, who am also an elder, and a witness of the sufferings of Christ, and also a partaker of the glory that shall be revealed: Feed the flock of God which is among you, taking the oversight <thereof>, not by constraint, but willingly; not for filthy lucre, but of a ready mind; Neither as being lords over <God's> heritage, but being ensamples to the flock. And when the chief Shepherd shall appear, ye shall receive a crown of glory that fadeth not away. (1 Peter 5:1-4)*

In this passage, we clearly see those who are commanded to *feed the flock*. These under-shepherds must take the oversight of the sheep, but they must do so with the proper motives outlined in these verses:

"Not by constraint, but willingly." This can be understood in two ways. First, if the passage is speaking to the under-shepherd that is feeding the flock, then it speaks of his need to avoid force-feeding them. Secondly, if the passage is speaking of the shepherd taking the oversight, then it is speaking of his need to do so *willingly*, not by coercion.

"Not for filthy lucre." One should never take the office of the under-shepherd due to covetous desire; gain is not godliness.

"Of a ready mind." One's mind is made ready by bringing their thoughts under the subjection of Christ. This is accomplished through faithful study of the scriptures and steady, fervent prayer for the flock.

"Neither as being lords over God's heritage." An under-shepherd must never become drunk with the feeling of power, one who feels the need to control by force and fear. This type of leadership is *never* the way of a true shepherd.

"Being ensamples to the flock." The best leaders lead by example, not by command. An under-shepherd can best lead his flock by showing his own submission to *his* shepherd.

Then, the Chief Shepherd shall appear. This, of course, is the Lord Jesus, and He is the Chief Shepherd. Knowing these, we understand that his under-shepherds are the target of these instructions. Now, it is very important that these under-shepherds never forget that the flock belongs to the Chief Shepherd. They are only stewards who have been placed in this position of leadership over the flock until the Chief Shepherd returns. It is for this reason that every under-shepherd should consistently speak to the flock about the Chief Shepherd. They need to be told who it is that they belong to, and they need to be reminded of His return. They need to understand that the message is from their Chief Shepherd, that their spiritual food is supplied by His sending, and the direction for the flock is given to His servant. Furthermore, the under-shepherd must keep in fellowship with the Chief Shepherd. All actions and programs must be sanctioned by Him before they are enacted. It is therefore crucial to the proper development of that flock that the under-shepherd strives to maintain the guidelines laid down in the rule book of the Chief. All of this must be done with the understanding that, one day, the chief *will* return, and at that time, the flock will be presented to the Chief Shepherd.

For I am jealous over you with godly jealousy: for I have espoused you to one husband,

that I may present <you> as a chaste virgin to Christ. (2 Corinthians 11:2)

That he might present it to himself a glorious church, not having spot, or wrinkle, or any such thing; but that it should be holy and without blemish. (Ephesians 5:27)

And you, that were sometime alienated and enemies in <your> mind by wicked works, yet now hath he reconciled In the body of his flesh through death, to present you holy and unblameable and unreproveable in his sight: (Colossians 1:21-22)

Whom we preach, warning every man, and teaching every man in all wisdom; that we may present every man perfect in Christ Jesus: Whereunto I also labour, striving according to his working, which worketh in me mightily. (Colossians 1:28-29)

It is an awesome responsibility for the under-shepherd to care for the Chief Shepherd's flock. They must feed them with the feed He provides, lead them in the direction He designs, shear the wool when He schedules it, and trim the hooves when He says it's time.

Everything that the under-shepherd does in relation to the flock is to be done under the Chief Shepherd's supervision and endorsement.

As I look at the present condition of our churches, I can't help but wonder if, over time, men have not determined in their own minds that the food that the flock was given was insufficient. So they changed the diet of the Word, they changed the music, and they changed the message. In doing so, the flock became *hungry*. Little by little, the true born-again believers have dwindled away in many of our religious institutions, and they have been replaced by a flock that does not belong to the Lord.

For there are certain men crept in unawares, who were before of old ordained to this condemnation, ungodly men, turning the grace of our God into lasciviousness, and denying the only Lord God, and our Lord Jesus Christ. (Jude 1:4)

These are spots in your feasts of charity, when they feast with you, feeding themselves without fear: clouds <they are> without water, carried about of winds; trees whose fruit withereth,

without fruit, twice dead, plucked up by the roots;
Raging waves of the sea, foaming out their own
shame; wandering stars, to whom is reserved the
blackness of darkness for ever. (Jude 1:12-13)

The Relationship between the Chief Shepherd and the
under-shepherd.

With this crucial truth before us, it becomes
imperative that the under-shepherds retain a close walk
with their Chief. I believe that, in order for this close walk
to persist, certain actions must be maintained. I would
like to focus on **Four** such actions in this section.

First, there must be a constant line of
communication between the Chief Shepherd and the
under-shepherd. This is more than a healthy prayer life,
this is a spiritual line whereby the under-shepherd is
open to the impression of his guide at all times. This can
only be established by a healthy relationship between
the two.

The under-shepherd cannot fulfill the desire or
design of the Chief Shepherd by attempting to

128

communicate with Him three times per week, or as many times as he is required to deliver a message to the flock. He must maintain a close walk with his Chief, even when he isn't preaching.

If this walk is ongoing, then the under-shepherd will find himself in constant contact with his Chief. He will speak with his Lord in casual settings, not exclusively in religious ones or even in personal prayer. As he walks along, as he is busy working, he will often speak with his chief, whether in his mind or out loud.

The constant need of the flock will put the under-shepherd in the field for most of his time. This position makes it necessary for the under-shepherd to receive instruction from his chief at a moment's notice. Put simply, he must be able to hear and receive instruction while in the midst of his work. If the under-shepherd is counseling, he needs instruction. If he is comforting, he needs instruction. He absolutely must be able to receive instruction while he is on the move.

Pray without ceasing. (1 Thessalonians 5:17)

Next, there must be a strong familiarity with the set parameters, methods, warnings, and instructions of the chief. These instructions are already set down in God's Word. They are written in His book, and they are not optional. While we will certainly be tasked with making decisions and following special instructions in unique situations, most situations are clearly dealt with in our Bible. Even those special circumstances will fall under something provided in the scriptures.

We *cannot* be lazy. We must apply ourselves to prayer and study. When I began my tenure as a shepherd of a literal flock, I realized that I needed knowledge. I gained this knowledge by reading books written by those who owned their own sheep. I learned what to do and what not to do. I learned what the sheep needed and what they did not need.

I learned that copper was bad for sheep. I did not need to purchase any feed that was high in copper due to its toxicity. This would kill the sheep. Not only did I need to know this, but I needed to *submit* to this. I did not have the luxury of deciding on my own if this was a rule that I should follow or not.

Our Chief has given us a rule book. We need to know what it says, and we need to submit to what it says. This is necessary if the flock is to thrive. I say thrive because that is what we should desire. However, if we don't take the Chief's instructions seriously, the flock won't even survive. If the under-shepherd doesn't learn what to do, and what not to do, then he will inadvertently kill the flock.

Thirdly, <u>there must be complete submission to the Chief.</u> There will never be a time when the input of the under-shepherd will add to the plan of the Chief Shepherd. Our chief does not need our opinions, He needs our *obedience*. To think that we under-shepherds might have something to add is to think that the Chief Shepherd missed something. He doesn't miss things.

I often see this occurring when men question the validity of the scriptures. When you hear or read such phrases as, "a better rendering would be" or "in the original text." Our chief does not need us to fix His book: He needs us to be familiar with His book.

This is also seen in the tendency of our church-leaders to incorporate modern means into the church's methods. I do not imply that we should not use present day advantages to further the gospel or to assist in feeding the flock, but I do state clearly that we should never sacrifice the clear instruction of the Chief in order to appeal to this present world!

For example, I do not believe it is wrong to use a projector as a visual aid in preaching or even in congregational singing. However, I do believe it is wrong to incorporate worldly music with a worldly beat into our singing just to draw a crowd. I could establish several reasons for this conclusion, but it can be concluded in this simple, *scriptural* statement: it is not the will of our Chief.

<This> I say then, Walk in the Spirit, and ye shall not fulfil the lust of the flesh. For the flesh lusteth against the Spirit, and the Spirit against the flesh: and these are contrary the one to the other: <ins>so that ye cannot do the things that ye would</ins>.
(Galatians 5:16-17)

Next, for us to retain a close walk with our Chief Shepherd, <ins>there must be a predetermined intent to obey the Chief, no matter the difficulty of the task nor discomfort of the sheep.</ins> It is often the case that a shepherd must perform certain tasks that are, without question, unpleasant. For a literal shepherd, this can range from assisting a ewe in birthing to dealing with some sickness or malady that could potentially harm the entire flock.

As I previously discussed, it is necessary for sheep to have their tails docked. The removal of the tail prevents the buildup of manure and parasites, which is healthy and vital for the sheep, but this comes by the way of an uncomfortable practice.

As outlined in the previous chapter, the docking process required that I place a band on a lamb's tail a few days after birth. This would cut off circulation to its tail, causing it to eventually fall off. At the moment of applying the band, the lamb would show great discomfort by falling on its side, circling around a crying, etd. I never enjoyed watching this, but I knew that the discomfort would fade and the lamb would be fine. I also knew that if I did not do this now, the lamb would either have to have its tail amputated later in life, or it would likely die from parasitic infestations. I did what needed to be done, despite discomfort. This is the responsibility of the under-shepherd.

I am troubled by present day leaders of our churches who are more concerned with what the sheep *want* rather than what they *need*. Some leaders are careful to retain the comfort of their flock, when often it is their *discomfort* that is needed. We must predetermine to do what's needed, what the Chief Shepherd demands of us, if we are to help His flock. To do anything else is to be derelict in our duties and unworthy of our position.

The under-shepherd as Protector.

Upon acquiring a few head of sheep, it became very clear to me that I would need to familiarize myself with the common predators of the flock. I was amazed at the many natural enemies sheep had. It seemed that sheep were susceptible to just about every other creature of the wild with a predatory nature.

I recall reading a report concerning a lamb that had been carried off by an eagle. I do not live in an area where there are an abundance of eagles, but I do live in an area with an abundance of *hawks*. That is also when I noticed that the hawk population had increased in the sky above my farm. I also realized that this increase occurred at the height of lambing season. In response to this sudden growth, I decided to introduce the migrant hawks to my shotgun. Although I couldn't kill them with this weapon, I managed to convince them that it would not be in their best interest to come near my flock.

Admittedly, the greatest threat to the flock did not come from the hawks. I began to study other predators, such as wolves and coyotes.. Again, I do not live in an area with an abundance of wolves, but coyotes are very common. It is an eerie feeling at night when the coyotes begin to howl... While there may only be a handful of coyote pups and parents crying, they make it sound like there are hundreds. Often I would go to the barn at night while this menacing sound reverberated across the hills to find my flock all standing at attention, shaking in fear. At these times, I would employ a two-step solution to remedy their fear.

The first step was <u>recognition</u>. I would go in the house and grab the biggest, loudest gun I owned. I would then go out into the field toward the sound of the threat and fire the weapon multiple times. The loud report of my gun would let the coyotes know that I could hear them, and that I was here to deal with them. I recognized their presence, and they recognized mine. You will never be successful by sticking your head in the sand. You must face the enemy in one way or another. If I had not alerted those devils to my protective presence, they would have come for the flock. You must accept the challenge of the enemy.

The second step was <u>comfort</u>. After giving notice to the predators of my presence, I would walk into the barn and make my way among the sheep. As I walked among them, I would speak words of comfort. "Do not be afraid. I am here. Nothing is going to get you. It's all right, the shepherd is here." As I would do this, one by one they would lie down. Starting with the leaders, those who had known me the longest, the sheep would lie down. The fear would subside, the lambs would curl up next to their mothers, and peace would come to the flock.

I have never seen a society more intent on avoiding the real issues than this present one! In politics, in education, in health, and in religious circles, we do not face the true problems before us. People don't seem interested in recognizing who our real enemy is, and we have failed to inform the enemy of our resistance. This is illustrated in the book of Acts, chapter nineteen when a group of silversmiths, led by a man named Demetrius, stirred-up an entire city into an angry mob to attack the companions of Paul. It was not until the town clerk spoke up that any rational through was exhibited in the account. The clerk, being concerned for the people of his town and the legal ramifications of their actions, called out Demetrius as the true cause of the problem. He put the real enemy on the defensive by showing him that he knew *who* he was and *what* he had done. He then let Demetrius know that he was there to oppose his actions. That was step one. Then he spoke to the people, exhorted them to be quiet, and sent them home. That was step two.

I have previously mentioned using a weapon to bring fear, recognition and understanding to those that would harm the flock. In regard to the spiritual application of this principle, the weapon is clearly our bible. When it comes to dealing with Satan and his minions, there is nothing more powerful than the scriptures! Scripturally speaking, the reference to the weapon of the shepherd is clearly seen in the life of David. In First Samuel chapter seventeen, we have the account of this shepherd slaying both a lion and a bear, and we know of the power in the sling he carried. Combine that with the reference to the rod and staff in Psalms chapter twenty-three, and we can see a clear picture of a warrior-shepherd: one who carries his weapon to defend the flock. The power is in the weapon itself, rather than the strength of the under-shepherd. Our chief has given us a two-edged sword, which is our means of defending the flock. Our ability to protect His flock is not in our own will, nor in our own strength. We must rely on the Word of God as our defense! Personal views have no power. Feelings of passion and injustice have no power. But if you put the Word of God on your enemies, you will find that it is an effective and powerful defense. As a pastor, or a teacher with a class of students, or maybe a youth leader with young people under your care, you must let the enemy know that you carry a weapon of power! Brandish it in the open, use it frequently, keep it sharp in your mind! You may see the hawks circling above, but if they are aware of your weapon, then they will think twice before coming in for a landing. If some enemy does have the audacity and nerve to come in for the kill, then do not hesitate to use your weapon as a means of defense. I think often we fear being too aggressive with an enemy or a vassal of the enemy, concerned that we might destroy them. However, the weapon of the under-shepherd is not one of destruction, but one of power against the three-fold enemies of man: the *Flesh*, the *World*, and the *Devil*. For the sake of the flock, *use your weapon*.

And take the helmet of salvation, and the sword of the Spirit, which is the word of God: (Ephesians 6:17)

For the word of God <is> quick, and powerful, and sharper than any twoedged sword, piercing even to the dividing asunder of soul and spirit, and of the joints and marrow, and <is> a discerner of the thoughts and intents of the heart. (Hebrews 4:12)

The under-shepherd as a Watchman.

Son of man, I have made thee a watchman unto the house of Israel: therefore hear the word at my mouth, and give them warning from me. (Ezekiel 3:17)

Take heed therefore unto yourselves, and to all the flock, over the which the Holy Ghost hath made you overseers, to feed the church of God, which he hath purchased with his own blood. (Acts 20:28)

To be a watchman means to be diligent and aware. If I learned one thing as a literal shepherd, it is that there is a constant threat to the flock lurking around every corner. I was amazed at the myriad threats that shepherds must deal with on a regular basis. There were threats both seen and unseen, from within and without. It became crystal clear that, without a shepherd, the sheep would *undoubtedly die*. There is no hope, *no hope at all* for a flock without a shepherd. Once we recognize that our Chief Shepherd leads the flock *through* His under-shepherd, then we must also conclude that a flock will not survive without an under-shepherd. As the steward of the Chief Shepherd, it is the responsibility of the under-shepherd to serve as a watchman for the flock. As a shepherd, I would often stand in the field and watch as my flock would mosey about the field in search for that special clump of orchard grass. Often a threat would arise, and they would never even know. I would deal with the danger before it ever reached them. This was my duty as their shepherd. There was so much to watch for, so many signs to consider... It is vital for the shepherd to be informed and educated concerning his enemies. You cannot be a watchman with your eyes closed! You must open them wide and recognize the dangers for what they are.

In a literal flock, <u>a shepherd must watch for signs of **hidden** threats</u>. These are those things that can be present and yet never seen on the surface. To deal with these threats, the shepherd must take a hands-on approach. Hidden dangers are revealed by the slightest of changes in the nature of the animal, such as sluggishness, depression, or possibly a tendency to distance itself from the rest of the flock. Often these symptoms are obvious, such as a sudden disinterest in the food provided by the shepherd. Other times they can be more difficult to identify, such as a slight limp or hesitancy in their gait that would not be noticed by anyone other than their shepherd. I have seen ewes walk around as if nothing was wrong while their foot was infected due to ventures into forbidden areas. Only through consistent examination can these sort of maladies be discovered.

under-shepherds: watch for subtle changes in the members of your congregation. Watch for those who exhibited interest at one time but now seem disinterested. Watch for those who once showed a strong fortitude and determination in their service but have now become lax and negligent. These are the ones who seem to be preoccupied to the point of complete distraction due to some hidden enemy of the mind. under-shepherds, do not ignore these tell-tale signs! At the very least, a word should be spoken, an offering of prayer, an expression of concern! Those who are dealing with such enemies certainly need prayer.

He must also watch for **hindering** threats within the flock itself. This has already been discussed in a former chapter concerning the Butting order. These sheep will hinder the growth of the flock by keeping the others in a constant state of unrest. The offending animal will go about butting the ewes that are resting and chewing. It does not intend for the flock to have any peace. Sheep like this often have something irritating them, such as some object stuck under their wool, or perhaps a sickness of the brain due to an internal parasite. The shepherd, and in the case of a church, the under-shepherd, must deal with the offending element if they want to get rid of the hinderance. If it is an irritation that can be dealt with properly, then he will do so. He will attempt to find the burr under the wool and remove it. If it is a sickness of the mind, then the shepherd will take steps to remedy it. However, this is a long-term procedure that involves separating the affected animal from the rest of the flock while administering some form of medicine. Sometimes, an under-shepherd needs to administer aid to an afflicted sheep individually, with care and discretion. Unfortunately, if a sheep cannot be helped, there are times when they must be separated from the flock.

He must watch for **hungry** threats to the flock. These are the predators that look at the flock and lick their lips. In this area, it is difficult to separate the human element from the spiritual element. I know that we wrestle not against flesh and blood, but often it is flesh and blood that desires to consume the flock. Of course we understand that there is an underlying power at work, but the threat is still real, and often physical. However, as has been stated, the enemies of the flock are threefold. They are defined by John as such:

For all that <is> in the world, the lust of the flesh, and the lust of the eyes, and the pride of life, is not of the Father, but is of the world. (1John 2:16)

I believe that you can categorize these three as the *Inward* enemy, the *Outward* enemy, and the *Upward* enemy.

The *Inward* enemy is the lust of the flesh, or the flesh itself. This is the old Adamic nature that is at enmity with the Spirit of God. The under-shepherd must constantly watch this enemy, as it desires to overrun the Spirit of God:

> *For they that are after the flesh do mind the things of the flesh; but they that are after the Spirit the things of the Spirit. For to be carnally minded <is> death; but to be spiritually minded <is> life and peace. Because the carnal mind <is> enmity against God: for it is not subject to the law of God, neither indeed can be. So then they that are in the flesh cannot please God. (Romans 8:5-8)*

> *For the flesh lusteth against the Spirit, and the Spirit against the flesh: and these are contrary the one to the other: so that ye cannot do the things that ye would. (Galatians 5:17)*

The *Outward* enemy is the world and is defined by John as the "lust of the eyes." This is illustrated in the Garden of Eden when Eve *saw* the tree, that it was good for food, pleasant to the *eyes*. Of course, these two work together to destroy the flock. The nature of this predator is *satanic*, meaning that the world is subject to the god of this world, and that is Satan. So he is the nature of the world. He is the influence of it, and all of its principles, ideas, and motivations are therefore *his*.

Beware lest any man spoil you through philosophy and vain deceit, after the tradition of men, after the rudiments of the world, and not after Christ. (Colossians 2:8)

In this passage, we are given four basic warnings concerning the dangers of the world: philosophy, vain deceit, traditions of men, and the rudiments of the world. We cannot allow the world to come into our flock and destroy it with its godless philosophies, vanities or vain deceits, its traditions of men that are dead and dry, or its rudimentary principles. These principles attempt to teach the world that the impulses of humanity are natural and that it is healthy to explore them. When these things come into the flock, destruction is on the horizon!

The *Upward* enemy is the Devil and is defined by John as "the pride of life." I use the term "upward" due to the pride that is involved. Of course, we understand the origin of all carnal pride is the Devil himself. Pride has been the bane, the death knell of many congregations. It has produced infighting and discontent that has taken such a hold that, for some, there was no going back. Pride was the influence in the hearts and minds of the Pharisees who compelled the people to cry "crucify him."

An under-shepherd must fight this predator within his flock. He teach his sheep to give *all glory* to the Chief Shepherd and warn his people not to think of themselves more highly than they ought. Beware of the individual that elevates himself or herself to the position of watchdog within the flock! I am not against a person in the church who desires to assist the under-shepherd in being a watchman, but often you get a creature that thinks themself above all others under the name of protection. The watchdog of the shepherd was a humble animal, one that always kept its eyes on the shepherd. It never moved of its own volition, always waiting for the shepherd's command . If there was a threat in the night, the watchdog would warn the shepherd with a bark. If the shepherd deemed it necessary, he would take the dog with him to investigate the threat. If not, the watchdog would sit. I think we can see the correlation between a watchdog and a true servant of the flock of God that genuinely desires to protect God's people and God's work. Be careful of the pride of life, the upward enemy that comes from the very spirit of Satan!

An under-shepherd needs to recognize these threats as hungry predators. They *desire* to destroy. They are not defensive enemies, but offensive. Their desire is to *hurt* the flock. The flesh, the world and the Devil form a threefold-front that is working in unity to bring down every congregation that serves the Chief Shepherd!

He must watch for **hazardous** threats. These are the dangers that occur when a sheep gets itself into a place or position of danger. There is an interesting passage in Galatians that I feel explains this present thought.

Stand fast therefore in the liberty wherewith Christ hath made us free, and be not entangled again with the yoke of bondage. (Galatians 5:1)

The yoke of bondage here is referring to the Old Testament rite of circumcision. He is telling them they have been set free, at liberty, from these things that are bondage. The interesting part here is in the words, "entangled again." Especially when considering sheep, this becomes very significant. The wool of a sheep is its natural covering. That natural covering is such that it wants to *grab* whatever it is near. In this passage, the apostle is telling the church of Galatia to stay away from the things to which they used to be in bondage, or else they will get *entangled again*.

When I first began to raise sheep, I learned the necessity of a good fencing system. This provided several things that were for the benefit of the flock. It allowed me to rotate my pasture, to know where the flock was at all times, and to prevent them from getting entangled and becoming bound, or in bondage. There were areas where the grass grew under the bramble and the briars. Although the grass looked good there, any sheep that stuck its curious head into the briar would not be able to pull it back out. Often I have been forced to cut away the wool on a sheep to free it from such bondages. Sometimes I would cut the brambles for a temporary fix, and the sheep would walk away with the bramble still entwined in its wool. This is the natural result of a sheep going someplace where it does not need to go. I have often wondered what the sheep would say if I asked it why it put its head in there. Would it say, "I thought I could handle it," or, "I thought I could go there and not get caught"? Of course it will get caught! A sheep's wool is *naturally* going to become entangled! How do we prevent such things? By keeping them away from it. Build fences that ward and warn-off the flock. Here again we see the importance of preaching more than the self-help, motivational messages of our present day: we need *warning* messages, we need *rebuking* messages and we need *reproving* messages in our churches!

I recall one particular animal that broke out, refusing to abide by the rules of the fence. It broke through the fence in order to reach an area that was forbidden. The sheep became so entangled that I could not pull its wool free from the fence. As a result, I was forced to cut the bramble loose at the root just to get her free. It was still a few months before shearing season, so I took the sheep to the barn and cut away as much of the bramble as I could. For the next few months, this sheep walked around with little reminders of its adventure sticking out of its wool for all to see. If you had walked up and seen her, you would have asked, "what happened to that one?" The answer would be, simply, "she went where she should not have gone, and it left its mark." It is only natural that the outer covering can get entangled with its surroundings. Therefore, we need to *avoid* the areas that will entangle us again to bondage! Just as the Galatians needed to stay away from the dictates of the old law, the drunkard that has been set free should stay away from the bar. The drug addict that has been set free should stay away from their old haunts. There is not one sheep that can stick its head back into these areas and come out unscathed: it will always leave it's mark.

We need to build fences of *preaching* to help our flocks to avoid such hazards. I do not believe that people realize the benefit of the Word in our lives, nor do they realize the detriment that a lack of the Word will cause. Although we cannot police our congregations to keep them away from such hazards, we can warn them. Such warnings, seasoned by the Holy Spirit and authorized by the written word, have *power*. These fences of the Word need to be strong, clear perimeters that the flock is very aware of. They need to hear the preacher declare that drinking is a sin. They need to hear the preacher declare that fornication is a sin. These words of warning are vital if the flock is going to avoid the hazards that will wound and mark them for life.

We must watch for the **helplessness** that threatens the flock. There are times when a sheep will somehow end up on its back, unable to set itself right. In the sheep industry, this is known as "casting." If this sheep does not receive assistance quickly, the gasses in its stomach will cause it to die. This is not something that the sheep intended to do, nor is it something that it did *wrong*, but rather a random series of circumstances caused this to happen. Perhaps it was a short, stocky sheep with a heavy fleece of wool, which pulled it over. Or perhaps it was heavy with lamb, and trying to lie on a hill, it wound up rolling into that position. Regardless, it wasn't necessarily the fault of the sheep that it wound up in such a dangerous position.

Sometimes due to the weight that a sheep bears, it gets down and cannot get back up on its own. It is the responsibility of the under-shepherd to watch for any sheep in this position, and our Chief Shepherd will help us have the discernment and ability to recognize it.

The fact that the sheep is not at fault here is significant. I remember one sheep that would grow a great pelt of wool, larger than her peers. She would simply carry it around until the time of shearing without complaint. She would not get out of the fence and get entangled, or stick her head where it did not go, but rather she would contentedly and faithfully follow the shepherd and bear her burden. Her walk would get slower, but she would walk on anyway.

Still, she would occasionally have a day when it was just too much, and she needed some help to get back up. So the very watchful shepherd must walk out into the field where she lay. He must sit her upright again, help her to her feet, stand near to keep her steady for as long as she needs, speak words of encouragement telling her that it won't be long until the burden will be lifted. Then he can watch her as she gains her second wind and walks back out with the rest of the flock. Brethren, it is dangerous to forget those that sometimes get helpless and need the assistance of the shepherd! I fear that we as pastors and under-shepherds wind up with all our attention focused on the rebellious, the fence testers, and we fail to notice the needs of those faithful ones who just keep walking and bearing the burden.

The Shepherd and his Equipment.

There are a few items that the shepherd must always keep with him, for they are vital to the welfare of the sheep. Although there are some items used by different shepherds in various climates, I will only deal with those we find in the scriptures and attempt to convey their significance, relevance and application.

First, we see the **Rod**.

Yea, though I walk through the valley of the shadow of death, I will fear no evil: for thou <art> with me; thy rod and thy staff they comfort me. (Psalms 23:4)

It's Making. The rod of the shepherd is a picture of the Word of God. It was around three to four feet long, depending on the design of its owner, and it was designed by the shepherd himself. First, he would find a young sapling and dig it up with the root intact. (This shows the beginning of the written Word of God. In the beginning of the Word, we see one man, Adam, who is the root of every human being that has ever been born.)

Next, the shepherd would cut off the roots, leaving a knob at one end about the size of a man's fist. (Here we see the flood. Just as the shepherd begins cutting all the roots away, so was mankind cut away due to his evil imaginations; but thank God that Noah found grace in the eyes of the Lord!)

After the shepherd cut off the excess root's, he would begin trimming the rod to his liking. He would take a little here and a little there until the shape of the rod suited him. (In this we can see the mighty hand of God reaching down into the land of Ur and calling Abram out from his kindred to make him a mighty nation. Slowly, and yet beautifully, the Lord began to trim away all the other nations of the world until he had the one that he wanted. As God gave Abraham and Sarah a son, we begin to see the divine plan of God take shape, just as the Rod of the shepherd would begin to take shape.)

Finally, after he is through trimming, the shepherd would take some nails or spikes and drive them into it. This is the completion of the rod. (And just as the nails completed the rod, it was the nails that held the Lord Jesus Christ that completed the plan of God for the redemption of man! When Jesus died on the cross, arose from the tomb, and ascended into heaven, he completely fulfilled all of the law and prophecy.)

Its use as a Weapon. It is not difficult to find passages that exhibit the word of God as a weapon of both offense and defense. Even in the list of the armor of God in Ephesians 6, we find the sword of the Spirit, which is the word of God, and in Hebrews 4:12, we are told that the word of God is quick, powerful, and sharper than *any* two edged sword. In its use, it will divide asunder the soul and the spirit, and it will divided asunder the joints from the marrow. Further support of this truth is found in the comparison of the believer as a soldier in 2 Timothy 2:1-3. It is significant to note that before the Apostle Paul tells Timothy to endure hardness, as a good soldier of Jesus Christ, he tells him in verse two to commit the things he has heard from Paul to faithful men who will be able to teach others.

Thus we see that the soldier of Jesus Christ is armed with the Word of God. There have been several men who have witnessed a shepherd throwing this rod with amazing accuracy. It is said that these shepherds begin to practice throwing it at a young age, and by the time they were ready to care for their own flock, the rod had become a natural part of their lives, an extension of their arm. Whenever a wolf or some other predator would draw near the flock, the shepherd would let fly this weapon and drive the danger away. In time, every predator in the area would learn to avoid the shepherd and the flock he watches over.

Our passage from Psalms 23:4 tells us the rod is a comfort to the sheep. We understand that the chapter is coming from the perspective of a sheep writing about his shepherd. The sheep sees the rod hanging from the belt of his shepherd, and he is comforted. I think there is a twofold application in this statement.

First, our Chief Shepherd is the Word of God, and He is our comfort. Both the living Word and the written Word brings great comfort to the flock of God. Of course, this is due to the promises, guidance, strength, conviction, and so much more that the sheep gain from His Word. However, we also understand that the Word is our protection, for it is also His weapon, His rod. As I have stated earlier, the three-fold enemy of humanity is the flesh, the world, and the devil. The Word of God through the person of the Lord Jesus Christ is our protection from *all three*. He will, through the leadership of the Holy Spirit, use the Word of God in our hearts and minds to protect us in this warfare. It is crucial that the believer understands that his ability to be an overcomer is not of his own will power, personal fortitude, or stubbornness: if he is going to be an overcomer, he is going to need the Word of God. Only by our faith in the Word of God, both the living and the written, will we obtain victory over all that is in the world.

Secondly, the under-shepherd that wields the Word of God will be a great comfort to their assigned flock. It is the delivery of the Word of God on a constant steady basis that will keep the wolves and devils at bay. The under-shepherd *must* recognize the difference between a sheep and a wolf in the congregation. The sheep find comfort from the rod of shepherd. They are comforted when the Word is put on their children, and they find comfort when the Word is put into their family. The sheep need to know that the Word of God will be applied to their storms, and to their sorrows.

I was reading a passage in 1st Thessalonians that is well known, and something became very real to me:

But I would not have you to be ignorant, brethren, concerning them which are asleep, that ye sorrow not, even as others which have no hope. (1 Thessalonians 4:13)

I realized this does not tell us *not* to sorrow, but not to sorrow as **others which have no hope**. At the time, I had some families that were sorrowing due to a loss in the family. I was able to stand before them and to declare that we who are believers are not to sorrow like the world does, because we, unlike the world, have **hope**. I took them down through the verses that reveal the rapture of the church and finished with the last verse of this chapter:

Wherefore comfort one another with these words. (1 Thessalonians 4:18)

As a weapon, the rod of the shepherd is always to be used against the enemies of the sheep, which are the enemies of the shepherd. In Acts 9:4, the Lord Jesus did not ask Saul why he persecuted the believers, but why he persecuted _Him_. Thus, we can clearly see and understand that the enemies of the sheep are the enemies of the Shepherd! It is against those enemies that the Word of God is used as a rod or a weapon. That being said, this rod is more than a simple weapon. It has many applications to the sheep and their enemies.

For example, the rod is not to be used against the sheep themselves. I know we have all heard the illustration of the shepherd breaking the leg of a wandering sheep, but in reality this would be very impractical. The sheep would have to be a lamb in order for the shepherd to be able to carry it around all the time, and the damage to the leg could set up infection and kill the animal. Furthermore, the shepherd could accomplish the same task of endearing the lamb to himself by simply constraining it without injury. I can neither confirm nor deny if this action is actually employed by middle eastern shepherds, but I doubt it. The rod in its function as a weapon is never designed to be against the flock, but rather to be used to fight off their enemies. To illustrate this, we can consider the means whereby the shepherd would examine his sheep. Often as they would pass by, he would employ the rod to separate the wool on their back. This would allow him to see if there were any parasites working under the wool. Thus, we see that although the rod is laid to the back of the sheep, it does not *hurt* them. It is not against them, but rather it is fighting the hidden enemies of the flock. Every true pastor understands the importance of applying the scriptures directly to their congregation, and every teacher to their students.

Our present day view of Christianity often suggests that we are to never be offensive, always defensive. This, of course, is ridiculous. Pastors have taken up this concept and attempted to present themselves as more approachable to the congregation.

Thus, they've discarded their suits for casual dress, the pulpit for a stool, and the preaching for motivational speaking. Rather than standing in authority, they stand with "suggested living." This kind of thinking disarms the shepherd from being able to protect the flock. He must be on the offensive against those things that would harm the sheep! If it is an upcoming election, he must be offensive and attack the enemies of Christianity with the Word of God. If it is a local law to be passed that undermines godly morals and supports riotous living, he must attack the enemies of the flock with the rod of the shepherd to protect his sheep!

A third application of the rod is as a weapon of *separation*. This can be seen from this passage in Ezekiel:

And I will cause you to pass under the rod, and I will bring you into the bond of the covenant: (Ezekiel 20:37)

This statement is used to illustrate a truth about the actions of the shepherds of that day. Literally, the shepherd would stand at the opening of the fold where his flock was staying that night and count them one-by-one as they passed under the rod. To put it more plainly, a true sheep comes through the door under the rod. Anything that would attempt to enter into the fold that was afraid of that rod would find a hindrance there. The picture is a wonderful one! I am visualizing a wolf that is standing off and watching as the sheep are entering the safety of the fold. The wolf's desire, his hunger, is to enter that fold and feast, but he is aware that, to do so, he must either go through the door or over the wall. To go through the door, he must pass under the rod and be accepted by the shepherd. To go over the wall, he will then be faced by the attack of the rod. Thus the enemy is hindered by the rod of the shepherd.

It is a Comfort in the Fold. As stated before, the shepherd would count his sheep at night by having them each pass beneath his rod. This was his way of knowing every creature that entered the fold. Only those who pass under the rod are his sheep; All others are thieves and robbers.

Verily, verily, I say unto you, He that entereth not by the door into the sheepfold, but climbeth up

some other way, the same is a thief and a robber.
(John 10:1)

There are three passages I would like to consider for this thought, and I believe that with them we can see the comfort of the rod of the Shepherd, the word of God.

It's associated with <u>Counting</u>.

And concerning the tithe of the herd, or of the flock, <even> of whatsoever passeth under the rod, the tenth shall be holy unto the LORD.
(Leviticus 27:32)

When we consider the tithe of the herd, we understand that the tithe belongs to the Lord. When we add that concept to passing under the rod, we understand that the counting of His property is dependent on the Word. Therefore, it is not the word of man that determines His property, but rather the Word of the Lord that determines His property. This is a great comfort. Put another way, I am not His because *I* say so, but because *He* says so! My assurance of heaven does not depend on the weak words of my own making. What a joy and comfort it is to have the Word of God as my assurance! I pass beneath the promises of assurance and am counted as one of His!

It's associated with Covenant.

And I will cause you to pass under the rod, and I will bring you into the bond of the covenant: (Ezekiel 20:37)

This is tied to the strength of the counting. Just as the counting of the sheep is dependent on passing under the rod, so is the covenant between the shepherd and the sheep dependent on the rod, or the Word of God. His promises are not only true: they are *eternally* true. This is the bond of covenant. I am just as assured of heaven right now as I would be if I was already there. This is solely due to the Word of God, because God gave His sheep His word. Again, we find comfort here.

Recall with me the account of the Abrahamic covenant in Genesis chapter fifteen. Abraham was commanded by the Lord to lay out before Him a sacrifice. He did so, and the Scriptures tell us how he divided them and laid them out. The Lord then put

Abraham into a deep sleep, which caused him to have a vision. That's when something truly wonderful occured:

And it came to pass, that, when the sun went down, and it was dark, behold a smoking furnace, and a burning lamp that passed between those pieces. In the same day the LORD made a covenant with Abram, saying, Unto thy seed have I given this land, from the river of Egypt unto the great river, the river Euphrates: (Genesis 15:17-18)

The act of covenant was accomplished by the two parties passing, or walking among the sacrifice. Often this was in a figure-eight, which represents infinity. Here we see a smoking furnace and a burning lamp. The smoking furnace was God the Father as he is seen coming down on the Mount Sinai.

And mount Sinai was altogether on a smoke, because the LORD descended upon it in fire: and the smoke thereof ascended as the smoke of a furnace, and the whole mount quaked greatly. (Exodus 19:18)

The burning lamp is God the Son. Of course, this is easily represented in the Scriptures. He stated clearly that he was the Light of the World. Now if we tie this in with New testament scripture, we can see a great, comforting truth:

> *For when God made promise to Abraham, because he could swear by no greater, he sware by himself, (Hebrews 6:13)*

If the new covenant had been between God and man, then it would depend on both parties to keep the specifics of the agreement. Man seems to have a problem doing this. However, the covenant was *not* made between God and man, but rather we see how that God swore by Himself! The new testament, the new covenant that assures us of our salvation, was between God the Father and God the Son; and God the Son is the Word of God! If we read further in Hebrews, this becomes even clearer:

> *For men verily swear by the greater: and an oath for confirmation <is> to them an end of all strife. Wherein God, willing more abundantly to shew unto the heirs of promise the immutability of his counsel, confirmed <it> by an oath: That by two immutable things, in which <it was> impossible for God to lie, we might have a strong consolation, who*

have fled for refuge to lay hold upon the hope set
before us:

Which <hope> we have as an anchor of the
soul, both sure and stedfast, and which entereth into
that within the veil; Whither the forerunner is for us
entered, <even> Jesus, made an high priest for ever
after the order of Melchisedec. (Hebrews 6:16-20)

It's associated with <u>Care</u>.

In the cities of the mountains, in the cities of
the vale, and in the cities of the south, and in the
land of Benjamin, and in the places about
Jerusalem, and in the cities of Judah, shall the
flocks pass again under the hands of him that telleth
<them>, saith the LORD. (Jeremiah 33:13)

The "telling" of the flock again refers to their
numeration. In this we see a reflection of John 10:

Verily, verily, I say unto you, He that entereth
not by the door into the sheepfold, but climbeth up
some other way, the same is a thief and a robber.
But he that entereth in by the door is the shepherd
of the sheep. To him the porter openeth; and the

sheep hear his voice: and he calleth his own sheep by name, and leadeth them out. And when he putteth forth his own sheep, he goeth before them, and the sheep follow him: for they know his voice. And a stranger will they not follow, but will flee from him: for they know not the voice of strangers. (John 10:1-5)

It is, of course, a natural and expected thing for a shepherd to know his flock by name. It is due to his closeness with them, his watch care and his familiarity, that he knows them and can "tell" them. In the telling of them, as each one would pass under the rod, he would call their name. This is a great comfort to the flock. As I pass under the Word of God, I am called out as one of His. I am a part of His sheep because I pass under the rod! I have not climbed up some other way: t Shepherd knows me, He counts me, He has covenanted for me and all is passed under the rod of comfort, the Word of God. My salvation is under the rod, my service is under the rod, my submission is under the rod, and my security is under the rod of the Word of God! This is my comfort.

<u>Next, we see the **Staff**.</u>

Yea, though I walk through the valley of the shadow of death, I will fear no evil: for thou \<art\> with me; thy rod and thy staff they comfort me. (Psalm 23:4)

The staff of a shepherd is well known in present society. We have all seen pictures of the long staff with the crook on one end. This staff is representative of the Holy Spirit working in the lives of the flock. It is the means whereby the Shepherd takes care of His sheep while traveling to and from the green pastures and the still waters. We must note that both the rod and the staff are a comfort to the sheep. As we have already determined, the rod represents the word of God, but the staff is a picture of the Holy Spirit. It is not difficult to find passages that teach of the comfort of the third person of the Trinity:

And I will pray the Father, and he shall give you another Comforter, that he may abide with you for ever: \<Even\> the Spirit of truth; whom the world cannot receive, because it seeth him not, neither

knoweth him: but ye know him; for he dwelleth with you, and shall be in you. (John 14:16-17)

The correlation between the staff in the lives of the sheep and the Holy Spirit in the lives of the believers can be seen in its use and its user.

The Shepherd and his staff. It is very important to understand that the staff is used by the shepherd. The sheep should not focus on the staff itself, but rather on the one who uses it for the benefit of the sheep. Those that focus on the staff are of such a nature that their view must be of "self." For instance, a shepherd must sometimes lead his sheep through dangerous areas. If the sheep would recognize this and focus on the staff itself, and what it's for, then the sheep would focus more on the fact that it was saved, rather than on the one who actually did the saving. Consider this simple fact: it is not the *method* that matters insomuch as the *master*. This broken mentality is found in such areas as your present-day "faith healers" who focus on the power of the "Spirit" rather than on the Savior himself. This is also evident in the focus of many churches on the the trials of life and deliverance from their storms, rather than on the deliverer Himself.

The Holy Spirit never intends to take the spotlight in our lives. He always desires to magnify and glorify the Lord Jesus Christ. He is not here of His own volition, but was sent here by the Lord Jesus and is working on his behalf.

Nevertheless I tell you the truth; It is expedient for you that I go away: for if I go not away, the Comforter will not come unto you; but if I depart, I will send him unto you. (John 16:7)

We must be wary of any religion or denomination that makes the Holy Spirit the focus of their worship, rather than the one who *sent* him. The staff does not glorify the staff, nor does it speak of itself; the staff reveals the arm of the one who uses it to benefit the flock.

Howbeit when he, the Spirit of truth, is come, he will guide you into all truth: <u>for he shall not speak of himself:</u> but whatsoever he shall hear, <that> shall he speak: and he will shew you things to *come. He shall glorify me: for he shall receive of mine, and shall shew <it> unto you. (John 16:13-14)*

The guidance of the staff. I am certain that we have all heard the stories of how a shepherd would lay the staff on the side of the sheep to guide them through the valley of the shadow of death. Honestly, I cannot speak of such things specifically, for I have not done this. However, when it comes to guiding sheep, I have been greatly assisted by the long, hooked shepherd's staff. The guidance of a flock involves much more than just leading them through areas of danger. The flock needs guidance in their every day lives.

Often I would gather my flock in a pen to walk them through a foot bath. This was to protect them from any infection that they might develop due to cuts and bruises in their hooves. This was always a difficult process, in spite of all the previous times that the flock had experienced it, and many of the sheep would look at the bath as if it were a lake filled with alligators. I would begin this process by taking the staff and laying it on the back of one of my mature ewes, which might have been old Kate or Big Momma, who always seemed to remain calm and have some sense about her. I would gently take the staff and bump them to get them moving, and so they would walk through the bath. This would show the others what to do. As this would occur, most of the rest of the flock would follow with nothing more than a gentle nudge or pull from the staff. However, there were always those who feared the imagined alligators. These would stand back against the gate. cringing in fear, until they would finally take off at a full run and jump the bath. I would then have to take the hook of the staff and pull them back through the bath. It is interesting to consider that these who would not trust the shepherd ended up having to walk through the bath *twice*. Some were even more stubborn still and would not go through the bath until I applied pressure with the staff, holding them low and guiding them through.

The lesson is clear. The guidance of the Holy Spirit often comes through nudges, impressions of assurance, even comfort to go forward in times of doubt. Furthermore, the view of watching those who have served the Lord faithfully for years gives proof of the guidance of the Lord through the Holy Spirit. Just as the younger sheep would follow as the older ones simply walked through due to the touch of the staff, so should believers follow suit. And what a great truth it is that we should be moved with only the *touch* of the staff! It is profound to consider the unnecessary roughness of the Shepherd on those sheep who refuse to have faith, who refuse to believe, and refuse to follow. Rather than simply walking through the bath in obedience, they jump, they pull, and they finally are forced to walk through by pressure as opposed to the nudge. What a lesson this should be!

The reach of the staff. The design of a shepherd's staff is useful for much more than simply nudging a sheep. If a simple push or nudge was all he needed, the staff could just be a long rod. However, the staff is designed to surround either the neck of a full-grown sheep or the torso of a lamb or yearling. This design is significant due to the use of the staff in its reach. Often sheep get themselves into areas where they should not go, areas of danger such as thorn bushes. Of course, where I live there really aren't many areas where a sheep easily could fall to its death, but there are plenty of brambles and thorns. This danger would arise often as sheep would become interested in the greenery of some thorn bush. It would begin to eat the leaves on the outer layer of the bush until they were gone then venture deeper for those it could not reach. Over time, the animal would end up with its entire body within the bramble. Many times, I have found sheep so tangled in these bushes that they absolutely could not get free. They were completely dependent on me to rescue them. And so I would take my shepherd's staff, reach into the area where the sheep was bound, wrap around its head and neck, and begin to pull. Sometimes it would take nothing more than a bit of pressure for the sheep to come free, but other times it would be much more difficult. The severity of the danger depends on the amount of time that the sheep has remained in the bush, and how far in it has traveled.

This is an excellent example of how people become entangled in the affairs of this world. We see how men can become enamored with the greenery of the world and begin to enjoy its fruit without going too far. However, it is the nature of man to desire more. The attractions of the flesh are never really satisfying. No matter how much you get, it will never be enough. This never-ending desire for more is what causes them to go *deeper*. I find it interesting how that man is able to ignore the pricks and pains that come as a result of their progress, just to get another taste. After all, alcoholism and drug addiction do not happen all at once. Addiction is gradual, beginning with just a simple taste. Over time, the desire for more brings about certain behavioral tendencies that produce pain by design. An alcoholic will drink to excess and hurt his family. A drug addict will become a funnel for money so that he might acquire his drug. This continues until the person becomes completely entangled by the sin. This is the image of *bondage*. Once they have gotten this far, it is only through the delivering power of the Lord, by the presence of the Holy Spirit, that man can be set free! The good intentions of our present day addiction programs will never be enough to truly set men free. The idea that "an alcoholic is always an alcoholic" is a very depressing concept. I wish to state to all that there is a freedom provided by our Great Shepherd! It is a supernatural work of the Holy Spirit in the hearts of men that fills the void within. Just as the staff of the shepherd reaches into the place of bondage and pulls his sheep free, so does the presence of the Holy Spirit wrap around the heart of the sin-sick soul and sets them free!

What a beautiful thing it is to see one set free from bondage. Unfortunately, this is often not the end of those who enter into bondage. Let's look to the words of James:

But every man is tempted, when he is drawn away of his own lust, and enticed. Then when lust hath conceived, it bringeth forth sin: and sin, when it is finished, bringeth forth death. (James 1:14-15)

In this picture the sheep is tempted by the greenery of the thorn bush. It is drawn away of its own lust. It is enticed or lured to venture into the area of thorns for the taste of the leaf. When the sheep gives in to its enticement, the lust is conceived. Now the sheep has committed a sin or a trespass. That which the sheep has done is against the will of the Shepherd, and that is a trespass. But what if the sheep never makes a sound, never cries out, but simply continues deeper and deeper into the bush? "And sin, when it is finished, bringeth forth death." What a terrible sight to behold when you find this poor creature hanging in a bush of thorns, dead from the torture of its bondage! How *horrible* to find men and women who have left this life in the grip of some lust, some addiction that they thought would not hurt them! How desperately we need the working power of the Holy Spirit to deliver men and women from the bondage of sin!

The comfort of the staff. This is something that the sheep are very familiar with.

Yea, though I walk through the valley of the shadow of death, I will fear no evil: for thou <art> with me; thy rod <ins>and thy staff they comfort me</ins>. (Psalm 23:4)

It is not difficult to speak of the comforting power of the Holy Spirit. Every true believer has felt this blessing at one time or another, and the picture of the staff being a comfort is also easily seen. The shape of the staff shows His power to <ins>envelop</ins> the believer. The length of the staff shows the power to <ins>reach</ins> the believer. The guidance of the staff shows the power to <ins>direct</ins> the believer. All of this speaks <u>comfort</u> to us! When I am in the midst of the storm, and His presence seems to come all around me, I am comforted. When I feel all alone, and His presence is able to reach me, I am comforted. When I do not know which way to go, and His presence gives me a nudge in the right direction, I am comforted! His guidance is not grievous, His reach is not invasive, His envelopment is not excessive: it is an essential need of the flock. We need His staff of comfort in our lives!

The Establishing of a Shepherd.

Every shepherd knows what it means to have the responsibility of the flock on his shoulders. A shepherd does not *become* a shepherd by just walking into the flock and saying, "Here I am, everyone follow me." I am afraid it is not that easy. There are some necessary things that a shepherd must do in order to establish himself as the shepherd of the flock. When I first began to build my flock, I enquired of other farms that might have sheep for sale. I found a few here and a few there, and over time I amassed the number I desired. Once I had purchased the sheep, they belonged to me, but the sheep did not *know* me. I took my trailer to their corral and loaded them up. I took them to my farm and released them into my barn, where they were again contained for a time. But before I released them onto the fields for grazing, I decided that they needed to recognize me as their shepherd. Thus, the relationship between myself and my sheep began to take form.

To cement myself as their shepherd, the sheep first needed to see me fulfilling the role of their shepherd. These are the necessary steps for forming this vital relationship:

First, you must <u>feed the sheep</u>.

So when they had dined, Jesus saith to Simon Peter, Simon, <son> of Jonas, lovest thou me more than these? **He saith unto him, Yea, Lord; thou knowest that I love thee. He saith unto him,** Feed my lambs. **He saith to him again the second time,** Simon, <son> of Jonas, lovest thou me? **He saith unto him, Yea, Lord; thou knowest that I love thee. He saith unto him,** Feed my sheep. **(John 21:15-16)**

First and foremost, the relationship between the shepherd and the sheep is introduced by the provision of the shepherd. Simply put, sheep must be fed. The base need of the sheep will entice them to approach the provision he gives. Put another way, sheep are willing to receive the provision before they fully trust the shepherd. Every new pastor should learn this. If he wants his congregation to trust him as an under-shepherd, then he must feed the sheep. The trust that is then built between the sheep and the shepherd occurs over time. As a literal shepherd, new sheep that I acquired would begin to associate me with their feed. With each day, they began to trust me more and more. After some time, they became less and less afraid, until one day they would rush toward me any time I entered the barn. Rather than waiting to eat, they would crowd around me desiring to be one of the first to get the feed. As they crowded around me, I made physical contact with the sheep. I would have to push them out of the way, and they eventually got used to my touch, my scent, and my voice.

Between us and our Great Shepherd, the trust is established at the moment of conversion, but his continued provision for us will strengthen and build that relationship throughout the believers' life. The longer we live, the more we will love Him. Each provision, each contact, each moment we spend with Him only makes us more familiar with Him, and that will cause us to love Him more. Each time we feast at the table of the scriptures, we see Him better. It matters not where you feast from in His Word, He is there.

Search the scriptures; for in them ye think ye have eternal life: and they are they which testify of me. (John 5:39)

Each time we sit at the table of worship, our intimacy with Him will grow. At those times when you enter into your closet of prayer, or you experience some moment of adoration in the house of God, your faith, trust, and love for your Shepherd will become greater and more established.

The quality of the feed should also be considered. In the case of us with our Chief Shepherd, or us in relation to the Lord Jesus, the quality of the feed gets better as our journey with Him continues. I have heard people refer to their moment of conversion as the height of their spiritual life, but that cannot be the case. Years ago, I heard an illustration by a preacher concerning the testimony of a small child. The child said that salvation gets "tweeter and tweeter, till it turn to tugar."

Of course, the meaning here is that the walk with our Chief Shepherd does not lessen in quality, but rather it grows. The scriptures become more meaningful and their truths more evident as we journey. We study the scriptures as we have been commanded, and we find the sweetness and strength that we need as the battle of life ensues. The wonderful companion of the Holy Spirit only becomes more intimate and more meaningful in this life with Christ. I must say that the moment of my conversion was only the beginning! The nourishment I receive now is *much* better, *much more* than my first taste of His goodness!

The under-shepherd should also employ this truth in the provision to his flock. As he goes before them with each service, he should endeavor to have something richer, something stronger, something sweeter to give. This quality of nourishment can *only* come through study and prayer. Trust me brethren: if you will apply yourself, He will provide! An under shepherd simply cannot be lazy. Your flock need the highest quality feed that you can provide. Read books, listen to sermons, meditate on passages, sit in some classes, and above all, *pray*! Give them more than the roughage, and give them more than sweet feed; Give them something that will cause them to grow and grant them the ability to face the world!

Secondly, you must <u>lead the sheep</u>.

The leadership of the shepherd is exclusive to himself. It is completely His realm and responsibility to be the leader. The comparison of physical sheep to the believers places us in the position to understand that sheep cannot lead sheep. This concept is equal to the blind leading the blind. I have watched the sheep in my pastures, and by doing so I understand that they do not *watch* where they are going. Without a shepherd, they do not know where to go, especially when something new is introduced into their lives. I certainly had some old faithful ones that had learned the location of the gap to a field, but this was after following my leadership for years. They could simply make their way to that gap and thereby lead others, but that knowledge was only due to my previous call. Sheep do not know what is best for them, they do not know where they need to go, and they do not know what they need to do. This is a fundamental truth that must be grasped by under-shepherds: sheep without a shepherd will perish.

Let the LORD, the God of the spirits of all flesh, set a man over the congregation, Which may go out before them, and which may go in before them, and which may lead them out, and which may bring them in; that the congregation of the LORD be not as sheep which have no shepherd. (Numbers 27:16-17)

This truth is further revealed by the forsaking of a hireling.

But he that is an hireling, and not the shepherd, whose own the sheep are not, seeth the wolf coming, and leaveth the sheep, and fleeth: and

the wolf catcheth them, and scattereth the sheep.
(John 10:12)

The application of this truth is pertinent to both the under-shepherds and the flocks. The under-shepherds are to understand that He leads us so we can lead them. This topic has already been addressed in a previous chapter, but it cannot be over-emphasized. As a pastor, I do not have the luxury of following the example of Elvis Presley and doing things "my way." I must follow the instructions that have been left to me by my Chief.

Furthermore, the flock needs to understand this same principle. Most of our church members have lost the principle of following. We are now dealing with ridiculous notions in the church, such as relative truths, enlightened views, and so on. The result of such unbiblical ideologies is that everyone simply does "their own thing." This is an extremely dangerous environment in the church! It is the same setting that we see at the end of the book of Judges:

In those days <there was> no king in Israel: every man did <that which was> right in his own eyes. (Judges 21:25)

It is also true that sheep need to be led, rather than driven. Their nervous nature will cause them to scatter when driven. However, for them to be lead is a calm exercise of trust that they are only willing to give to their shepherd. Now, to establish this position as their leader, the shepherd is going to need to practice these two things:

1. The under-shepherd must associate a call with provision. In the flock that I acquired, I developed a specific call that I used consistently whenever I wanted to lead the sheep into pasture. If I was going to open the door of the barn to allow them to graze, I would begin my call as I approached the barn. At first, the new sheep would be skittish and nervous, but over time they began to understand that this call meant one thing: it was time to graze in green pasture. We who are believers have come to understand this about our Chief Shepherd as well. Where He leads us, He feeds us. He provides not only our sustenance, but also green pastures for us to feast on. Equally so, a pastor needs to develop a call to his people as they gather to sit under his voice. They need to know that he is leading them into green

pastures. He has prepared the pasture with study, cleaned the pasture of the foreign materials of the world like human opinion or personal agenda, and he is now going to give them the good Word of God. There should be an attitude of trust and expectation when the congregation hears the call of their under-shepherd when he says "turn with me in your bibles." This phrase shows that the pastor is *leading* them rather than *driving* them. "Turn with me" implies that, before he takes them there, he has already been there.

2. The under-shepherd must actually *lead* them, not just *send* them. Our Lord has exemplified this in a magnificent way.

Seeing then that we have a great high priest, that is passed into the heavens, Jesus the Son of God, let us hold fast <our> profession. For we have not an high priest which cannot be touched with the feeling of our infirmities; but was in all points tempted like as <we are, yet> without sin. (Hebrews 4:14-15)

Here we understand that wherever the Lord Jesus leads us, he has already been there. And not only has he already been there, but he has made a provision for our wellbeing.

There hath no temptation taken you but such as <is> common to man: but God is faithful, who will not suffer you to be tempted above that ye are able; but will with the temptation also make a way to escape, that ye may be able to bear <it>. (1 Corinthians 10:13)

An under-shepherd must also be such a leader. It is not sufficient for the pastor to tell people to be a witness; he must be one as well. He must be willing to lead in all aspects of the ministry. It is my belief that a pastor should lead in physical work at the church if he expects his members to work at the church. He must be willing to do the menial jobs to lead the congregation in service. Pastors cannot drive their congregations to serve, they must lead them into service! We cannot drive them into standards, we must lead them into standards! We cannot drive them into bible knowledge and study, we must *lead them* into bible knowledge and study! Pastor: you must do these things, and you must do them *with joy*. This work ethic and leadership is absolutely necessary if you ever hope to produce trust in the congregation.

Feed the flock of God which is among you, taking the oversight \<thereof\>, not by constraint, but willingly; not for filthy lucre, but of a ready mind; Neither as being lords over \<God's\> heritage, but being ensamples to the flock. (1 Peter 5:2-3)

Thirdly, you must <u>protect the sheep</u>.

I am the good shepherd: the good shepherd giveth his life for the sheep. But he that is an hireling, and not the shepherd, whose own the sheep are not, seeth the wolf coming, and leaveth the sheep, and fleeth: and the wolf catcheth them, and scattereth the sheep. The hireling fleeth, because he is an hireling, and careth not for the sheep. (John 10:11-13)

Over time, my flock learned that my presence ensured their safety. They came to understand that I would not hurt them, and that the howl of the coyote was not a threat if I was in the stall. It was interesting to note that my voice in the barn would override the voice of the predator outside. And so, on those cold nights when the lambs were being born, I would walk through the barn speaking to the flock. Over the bluff was a den of coyotes that would ring out their eerie cry in unison. This sound would reverberate off the rocks of their den in such a way that it sounded like they were right outside the barn. Those days when the coyotes would start up before I came to the barn, I would find the flock huddled up in the back. On those nights, I would speak to them, and they would be comforted. The huddle would break up, the ewes would lie down, the lambs would climb up on their mothers backs or curl up close beside them, and all would then be at rest. They understood that the predators voice had no power over the shepherd's voice! I was there to protect them. Surely we can see the correlation here between this illustration and the voice of our Lord? Often we will find that the calming words of the scriptures override the cries of the predator, even when it seems to be right outside the door. What comfort comes from the still, small voice of the Holy Spirit! We know that, if He is with us, then He will protect us.

Of course, we understand that this also applies to the under-shepherd. A congregation should always know that their Pastor will protect them. A pastor's first priority in his ministry should be the flock, not his own personal promotion. Often we find men who become more interested in their own ministry than they do the flock of God. Never leave the sheep and allow the wolf to catch them, scatter them, and kill them! It is the hireling that flees, and that is because he does not care for the sheep, but only for himself. The Apostle Paul understood this, and when writing to the church of the Philippians, he told them that he wanted to send Timotheus to them due to his trust and faith in his pastoral abilities. Paul makes a statement in chapter 2 verses 21-22 that I feel are very relevant and prevalent in our present day:

For all seek their own, not the things which are Jesus Christ's. But ye know the proof of him, that, as a son with the father, he hath served with me in the gospel. (Philippians 2:21-22)

Paul says, "for all seek their own, not the things which are Jesus Christ's." In this present day, I am seeing a group of preachers who are more interested in furthering their own ministry, building a following, and getting a name for themselves than they are in seeking the things which are Christ's! This is the very definition of a *hireling*. Their interest is not in the well-being of the flock or flocks of God, but rather in furthering their own personal agenda or brand. Here we see Paul stating that Timothy has proven himself by being a *servant in the gospel*. Furthermore, he states this after referencing those who "seek their own." Our congregations need to know that their under-shepherds are not seeking their own, but rather that they are caring for the flock.

The elders which are among you I exhort, who am also an elder, and a witness of the sufferings of Christ, and also a partaker of the glory that shall be revealed: Feed the flock of God which is among you, taking the oversight <thereof>, not by constraint, but willingly; not for filthy lucre, but of a ready mind; Neither as being lords over <God's> heritage, but being ensamples to the flock. And when the chief Shepherd shall appear, ye shall

receive a crown of glory that fadeth not away. (1 Peter 5:1-4)

<u>The Experience of the Shepherd</u>.

First of all, a shepherd must be familiar with the landscape. It is the shepherd's job to know where to find the green grass. He must know where the still water is in order to keep the sheep from walking into a rushing stream. He must know which path is safest and where the predators will lie in wait. When we consider all of the responsibility that this places on the shepherd, surely the question must arise in our minds: "how can a shepherd know all of these things?" There is only one way: he must go to these places himself before he can ever lead the flock there. He must walk over all of the fields. He must wade into the streams. He must climb all of the mountains. It is through his own experiences that a shepherd knows where to lead the flock. How beautiful a picture this paints for us of our Savior, and what joy it should give us when we consider his leadership! No matter where He lead's me, I know that He has already been there before me. No matter what I go through, I know that He has already experienced it! Just as the three Hebrew children found Him in the fire, just as Daniel found him in the lion's den, I know that He has already gone ahead and made a way of escape for me. Praise be unto the Lamb of God! Even when He takes me over the rocky terrain of the mountains, and I can't see any relief in sight, I can trust that there is green pasture at the end of this journey; for I know that he has already been there! However, it's more than the knowledge that He has already been there that gives me comfort: it is the understanding that while I am going through the rocky places, He is walking again with me through my time of trial. He knows how to make it through, and He will never leave me. He most certainly has not promised me that I would not have to go through the hard places, but He *has* promised me that He will not leave me nor forsake me during those times. Too many of our present-day Christians want their Shepherd to keep them out of the hard places, but that is simply not realistic. We all must face these trials in life. Take comfort brethren that your Chief Shepherd knows where you are, He knows what you're going through, He knows what's ahead, and He knows what He is doing!

As for the under-shepherds, Paul understood the need for a bishop to have some experience under his belt. He specifically instructed Timothy that a bishop should not be a novice.

Not a novice, lest being lifted up with pride he fall into the condemnation of the devil. (1 Timothy 3:6)

Just as Timothy first placed himself under a pastor and served in the gospel with him for a time, so should all young preachers. It doesn't matter if that young man is going to serve in the pastorate or some other field, such as a traveling evangelist or a missionary, he will need to learn from the feet of an experienced and faithful pastor. I would even suggest that a young pastor who is now placed in the position as an under-shepherd continue to glean and learn from those who have already traveled down the road that he is now on.

Of course, it is true that no matter how long a man has been in the ministry, and no matter how far he has traveled or how much he has seen, he cannot know the answer to every question he is asked by his congregation. It simply is not possible for his experiences to cover all circumstances or situations, and thankfully so. There are people that approach me with problems that I do not have, I have not had, and I do not want. I have not walked where they are walking, and I have not felt what they are feeling. And yet, I am still able to pastor them, because I know someone who *does know* what they are feeling and *does see* where they are walking! It is essential that an under-shepherd lean on the Chief Shepherd's expertise and wisdom rather than their own. This understanding comes with years of service in the ministry. Many young men will be quick to offer some word of remedy that will either be ineffective or even damaging, when what people really need is to be directed to the Lord! Furthermore, a novice is not necessarily a young person, but rather a person who is newly planted in the church. I will state that young men, especially the extremely young, are not as equipped to handle the office of a bishop as well as one who has some years under their belt. That being said, accumulation of years does not automatically equip a man for the responsibility of leadership. I think this understanding is greatly needed in our day. Many of the churches I have been affiliated with have placed men in positions of leadership due to either their influence in the community or their financial status. Their knowledge of the scriptures was not a factor, nor was their spirituality. Because of this, churches have been led by the wisdom of the world rather than the wisdom of God, and thereby they have gone toward worldly ways. These churches have left the leadership of the Chief Shepherd and are now following hirelings that have their own agendas. Our churches need Spirit-filled men who know how to follow their Chief Shepherd, or else the sheep will scatter.

Secondly, a shepherd must be familiar with the elements. By the look of the sky and the feel of the air, a true shepherd will know when a storm is approaching. There are times when the shepherd needs to quickly get his flock to shelter before the storm hits. A flock that is overtaken by a storm will panic and scatter, causing injuries and death to the weak and the young. This is why the shepherd must know the weather and the elements around him. If he does, he can detect the storm and make preparations before it's too late.

I am sure that we will have no difficulty in seeing the working of the Savior in this example. What a comfort it is to know that nothing takes Him by surprise! He knows what lies ahead for His children, and He prepares us for it. Quite often I have found myself going through trials and troubles that I could not understand. As we often do, I would question my circumstances and struggle to understand why this would be happening to me. And then, sometime later, a storm would arise that I did not expect. It is at those times that I realized the Lord had been preparing me for that very storm. I was prepared for it as a result of the trial that He had just taken me through. If you are experiencing troubles and trials that you do not understand, remember that the Shepherd could be preparing you for a storm that's heading your way. This principle can be clearly seen in the scriptures:

My brethren, count it all joy when ye fall into divers temptations; Knowing <this>, that the trying of your faith worth patience. But let patience have

<her> perfect work, that ye may be perfect and entire, wanting nothing. (James 1:2-3)

The trying of the faith causes a work of patience. Patience then performs a perfect work in the believer that will leave them *entire*. This word means to be left complete, perfectly sound in both mind and body. It ends with the believer wanting nothing and needing nothing. So by this, we can see how the Chief Shepherd will prepare us using trials and make us able to face what is ahead. This is because He *knows* what is ahead.

As I consider this thought, I remember seeing a storm approaching while my sheep were out on the field. I would go quickly and call them up to the barn. The seasoned ones one would begin to make their way to me with a calmness that spoke of their trust, while the younger ones would show nervousness and fear at the sound of the thunder or the crash of the lightning. There were times when all of the flock would come up except for a few who had been taken with fear. I would put the flock in the shelter of the barn and then go out into the storm to gather the remaining few. I would always find them huddled under some tree or bush, shaking in fear and poorly sheltered. They did not realize it, but their covering would not protect them from the storm. They did not need to separate from the flock, and they should not have ignored the call of their shepherd. Once I had found the separated sheep, I would calm them, perhaps even take some feed to them, and then lead them back to the rest of the flock.

The lesson here is all so clear. Too often people allow storms to separate them from the church. Even some internal problem within the flock can cause a member to separate themselves and huddle under the shelter of pride or self-imagined righteousness. "Shelters" such as these that will not protect them from the damage from the oncoming storm. It is the job of both the Chief Shepherd and His under-shepherd to call the sheep into the fold at these times. When that call is rejected, the result is often loss that brings nothing but sorrow. Our congregations must be able to trust those who are given the rule over them, understanding that they care for their well-being and desire for them to be whole.

> *Obey them that have the rule over you, and submit yourselves: for they watch for your souls, as they that must give account, that they may do it with joy, and not with grief: for that <is> unprofitable for you. (Hebrews 13:17)*

It's not only the storms that the leaders must be familiar with, but all the elements. The shepherd needs to recognize when the day will be too hot for the flock to be out grazing, so that he can provide a cool place to rest until the heat of the day passes. He needs to know when the fields are too wet for the sheep to be walking in, due to their tendency to get foot rot after an over exposure to such conditions. He needs to know when the tender grass first begins to shoot forth from the earth in the spring, so that he can limit their grazing time to avoid certain toxicities until they become accustomed to the new growth. With the familiarity of the elements, and the watchfulness of a shepherd, he is able to avoid some of the problems that might otherwise arise amongst the sheep.

It is vital that the under-shepherd is capable of looking ahead and predicting certain dangers to the congregation. Recently I spoke with a pastor who was guiding his youth leader concerning an upcoming youth trip. The youth leader was not going to have room for all of the youth, and so he was considering picking some who could go on this turn, and perhaps then later allowing the others to go. The Pastor warned the youth leader of the dangers of this move. Although the trip was a good one, and would be helpful to those that could go, the damage that could be done by purposefully leaving others behind would be more than the benefit to those who went. The under-shepherd looked ahead, saw the potential for damage to the flock, and avoided it as he should. Even at times when things look like they are good, it takes a leader who is familiar with his surroundings to see the true signs of danger.

Thirdly, concerning the experience of the shepherd, he must be familiar with his flock. The Lord knows His flock. That is most certainly a true statement. The scriptures testify of this fact. David was aware that the Lord knew him.

(To the chief Musician, A Psalm of David.) O LORD, thou hast searched me, and known <me>.

Thou knowest my downsitting and mine uprising, thou understandest my thought afar off. Thou compassest my path and my lying down, and art acquainted <with> all my ways. For <there is> not a word in my tongue, <but>, lo, O LORD, thou knowest it altogether. (Psalm 139:1-4)

Let's consider the specifics of the Lord's knowledge found in these verses. First, He has searched me and known me. This speaks of a penetrating gaze, an examination that comes through an intent watchfulness. Although I am certain each of us would state that the Lord knew us before we were born, David here states that He has been watching me, and He knows the real me due to His watchfulness. I certainly would not argue with the Lord's sovereignty, but it is good for us to be aware that He is watching us always. I believe it is important for His under-shepherds to also employ this watchfulness. You need to know the *real* sheep over whom you have the watch-care! *Leaders need to pay attention*.

He then states that the Lord knows his down-sitting and his uprising. This could refer to his time to sleep and his time to awake. In that view, David says that the Lord is watching him when he goes to sleep, and the Lord is watching him when he wakes in the morning. It could refer to the places he sits, or rests, or dwells in life. If so, he is aware that the Lord knows of his haunts, the places where he prefers to spend his time.

I am the good shepherd, and know my <sheep>, and am known of mine. (John 10:14)

My sheep hear my voice, and I know them, and they follow me: (John 10:27)

He must know and understand all of the needs of his flock if he is to be a true shepherd. I would also like to point out that a shepherd not only knows and understands the needs of the entire flock, but he also knows the needs of each individual sheep. He knows each ewe, a mother sheep, that is with lamb, and how far along she is. He knows each lamb and what type of food it is eating. We can see that a true shepherd is familiar with each individual sheep underneath his care.

This fact speaks of a personal relationship that the sheep have with their shepherd. Just as this applies to the flock in the pasture, so does it apply to the flock in the church. The Lord Jesus not only meets the needs of the entire congregation, he also deals with each of His children individually. I must say that I am troubled with the mentality of our church members today. It would appear that many people are claiming to be saved, and yet they know nothing of a daily walk with the Savior. Salvation is only the first step to being a child of God. After a person is saved, it is then that this person begins to learn about their Savior. Every day after that will be a learning experience with the Lord! It was the Lord himself who said:

For whosoever shall do the will of my Father which is in heaven, the same is my brother, and sister, and mother. (Matthew 12:50)

How true this is! Whenever I need a brother to stand by me, He is there. Whenever I need the love of a mother, He holds me and rocks me in His love and grace. I thank God for my personal relationship with my Shepherd! Without it, I would be a most miserable creature. Friend, if your experience of Salvation did not thrust you into a personal relationship with the Savior, then there is a great possibility that what you experienced was counterfeit, and not a true conversion!

Of course, this also points to the responsibility of a pastor. One of the most difficult things that I have experienced as a pastor is seeing to the needs of each member of my church. But I believe that a true pastor will do his best to give each member equal time and attention. It is wrong for a pastor to pick out his "pets" and neglect the rest of the flock. However, it is important for me to recognize just how easy it is for a pastor to do this, and quite often unintentionally. There are many times when a pastor will get caught up in the problems of a particular member who does not mind sharing their needs while some other member, who is more reserved, is greatly in need of his attention. Although I do not have a formula or fail-safe answer to go by, I do believe that God will help us, as pastors, to see the needs of our flock if we will just stay near Him and keep our eyes open.

There is also the plague of personality. There are some people with dynamic personalities who are easy to get to know and be around, while there are others who are more introverted and shy. Although a pastor may feel awkward around some of his members, that is not an excuse to avoid or shun them. And even though a Pastor does not have all the answers to the questions that a member may have, it is important for the flock to know that the under-shepherd is there for them. And so, pastors, I urge you to be observant and prayerful over each and every one of the members that God has placed in your care!

A pastor also needs to be familiar with the instincts of a sheep. While any shepherd in the field will gladly point out that sheep do not maintain a lot of reasoning, they would also admit that sheep possess instincts of their own. Truly, sheep are not deep thinkers. When a sheep acts, the act does not come from a plan or strategy, but rather it comes from its natural instincts. A shepherd must understand this is he ever hopes to be successful with his flock. If he tries to make his flock do something that goes against their instincts, he will probably not get the job done. A good shepherd knows that the best way to accomplish his tasks is to use the natural behavior of his sheep to his advantage.

This is one reason why many pastors have trouble keeping a church. When will we ever learn that leading a church does not mean that we have to completely change everything about that church? Pastors need to learn to use the resources that are already present when they take the church! As an example, I would like to use the subject of supporting missions. There are many churches that have never supported a missionary. This does not necessarily mean the church is bad. It could simply be that they have never been exposed to the blessings of that particular ministry. If a newly called pastor tries to force his congregation into supporting a missionary, it is likely that they will rebel on him and, as a result, dissension will occur in the flock. I feel the proper way to lead a congregation into mission work is to first expose them to some missionaries. After a considerable amount of exposure has taken place, the instinctive reaction of the congregation will be to *get involved* with this work. In the terms of a shepherd, "sheep must be led, not driven." There is also the problem of "how we do it." I have witnessed many pastors getting upset over how they do it, versus how he wants it done. Let's be perfectly honest here. What does it matter if the church takes up the offering with ushers, or passes by the altar and drops their offering in? As long as the offering is taken, who cares how they do it! Remember pastors: it is not our job to conform a church into what *we think it should be*. Our job is to take the church as it already is and use its resources for the upbuilding of the church, and the Glory of the Lord! It is in this manner that we will see people working together and sinners being saved. Of course, all of this must be under the canopy of the scriptures, and if a pastor is faced with some tradition or "way" that is contrary to the Word of God, it will be necessary for that to change. But even in those times, an under-shepherd must be wise and take it slow to allow the flock to acclimate to the new leadership.

CONCLUSION

I suppose that there are a lot of so-called shepherds in
this world. In all walks of life, you can find leaders of
groups and people that hold the title of a shepherd in
some way. However, this role is one that is not easily
filled. Human leadership based on human understanding
is never sufficient in meeting the needs of their followers.
Man needs a shepherd that is *more* than himself. We do
not need another sheep to lead the sheep, we need a
Shepherd, a Good Shepherd, a Great Shepherd, a *Chief
Shepherd*. Even the under-shepherds are completely in
the dark without their Chief. I conclude, therefore, that
those who are not following the Lord Jesus are nothing
more that sheep, wandering around without any true
direction. They are hungry, ravaged by the elements,
and in danger of the predator. It is an elemental truth that
we need a shepherd. It is also a great truth that a

212

shepherd is available. One who is not a hireling, but a *true* shepherd. He loves His sheep, He knows His sheep, and He gives His life for His sheep! To the followers of this Shepherd I say: **Love Him in Return**. Trust Him, thank Him, and serve Him for all of your days. And to those who are unsaved, I say: give your life to this Shepherd. For He will never leave you, He will never forsake you.

End.

** All scripture references are from the King James Version.

ABOUT THE AUTHOR

Doctor Tim Shirley is the pastor of New Water Baptist Church in Summersville, KY. He has served as the under-shepherd for the same congregation for more than 25 years. He graduated with a doctorate in Theology from Grace Baptist Bible Institute in 2018.

He is happily married to his wife Lisa, with whom he has three children: Paul, Caleb, and Hannah, all of whom are now married and active in the ministry. His family has grown now to include four grandchildren: Peyton, Link, Josiah, and Ada.

In addition to his pastoral duties, Bro. Tim is the president of Beulahland Baptist Camp in Summersville, KY. He also serves as the Vice President of the Canaan Baptist Bible College from Jamestown, TN.